GOLDFISH AND ORNAMENTAL CARP

Bethen Pénzes
István Tölg

GOLDFISH AND ORNAMENTAL CARP

34 Color Photographs
57 Drawings
10 Tables

BARRON'S

Cover (upper photo) Telescope eye and veiltail by B. Kahl. (Lower left) Young redcaps by B. Kahl; (lower center) common domestic goldfish by Peter Lewit; (lower right) calico oranda by B. Kahl.

Technical advisor: Dr. Jürgen Lange, Berlin
Illustrations: Peter Lewit
Photographs: B. Kahl, p. 25, lower; pp. 26, 35; p. 36, upper and lower left; pp. 45, 55; p. 56, upper and lower left; pp. 65, 96; and from the authors' files

First English language edition published in 1986 by Barron's Educational Series, Inc.

© 1983 Eugen Ulmer GmbH & Co., Stuttgart, Germany.

The title of the German edition is *Goldfische und Zierkarpfen*

All inquiries should be addressed to:
Barron's Educational Series, Inc.
250 Wireless Boulevard
Hauppauge, New York 11788

Library of Congress Catalog Card No. 87-7382
International Standard Book No. 0-8120-5634-5 (H)
International Standard Book No. 0-8120-9286-4 (P)

Library of Congress Cataloging in Publication Data

Pénzes, Bethen.
  Goldfish and ornamental carp.

  Translation of: Goldfische und Zierkarpfen.
  Bibliography: p.
  Includes index.
  1. Goldfish. 2. Ornamental carp. I. Tölg, István.
II. Title
SF458.G6P46413 1986   639.3'753   85-7382
ISBN 0-8120-5634-5

PRINTED IN HONG KONG

456   490   98765432

CONTENTS

PREFACE

Of all animals kept only for pure enjoyment, goldfish were the first to be adopted as pets by humans and to be bred, refined, and cultivated. Goldfish originated in China, and their history as ornamental fish spans more than a thousand years. Today, they are appreciated more than ever. One of the main reasons for their new-found popularity might well be the desire for simplicity, a desire we are expressing in many facets of our modern, high-tech, highly complicated lives. Goldfish symbolize that sort of simplicity among aquarium fish. At the same time, the numerous, often quite dissimilar, varieties of goldfish fulfill a hobbyist's need for diversity and for a wide range of rearing methods. These fish can be raised in aquariums, in simple glass containers, in ceramic bowls, and in ornamental garden pools.

The history of ornamental colored carp, or koi, is less complex than that of goldfish, but in terms of popularity, carp can easily compete with their smaller relatives. Because carp grow quickly, attaining a weight of several pounds (1 or 2 kilograms) in only a few years, they are primarily fish for ponds and very large ornamental tanks. In these environments large, multicolored ornamental carp appear as patches of color in slow, easy, continuous motion. Koi were first bred and cultivated in Japan. Their introduction to western cultures did not occur until the early 1950s, but the number of koi enthusiasts has increased steadily ever since.

In 1965 we had the good fortune to observe goldfish breeding establishments in China firsthand. We studied the work of breeders, and their carefully developed breeding techniques, which are based on centuries of experience. While there we experienced firsthand the amazing intuitive understanding the Chinese have for their fish. What most impressed us was the meaning goldfish have for them: a true bond between human and fish. Even the poorest of the Chinese enjoy keeping goldfish, which satisfies them in much the same way as an expensive aquarium pleases more affluent Westerners.

Since our trip to China we have become increasingly involved in goldfish cultivation. In the course of this labor of love we have also become quite familiar with koi, and for several years now we have been keeping and breeding koi as well as goldfish. Both species offer new and interesting experiences to anyone who enjoys large coldwater ornamental aquariums or garden ponds.

The primary purpose of this book is to provide ideas and helpful tips to hobbyists interested in these colorful Far Eastern fish, and to discuss various aspects of their care and breeding. We sincerely hope that we have succeeded and that our readers will derive as much pleasure from goldfish and koi as we have over the last twenty years.

Budapest, Spring 1983   Bethen Pénzes
                               István Tölg

GOLDFISH

INTRODUCTION

Goldfish are by no means a new addition to the aquarium hobby. At the turn of the century goldfish were very popular; in fact, keeping goldfish was a fad. They were kept in marble basins and decorative fountains in homes and gardens, as a typical expression of the spirit of the times. Goldfish breeding was directed toward developing long, fragile veil-like fins similar in appearance to the silky, soft, flowing textiles in fashion during those years. When the taste for elegant fragility went out of style, the popularity of goldfish waned as well. The rapid development of modern aquarium technology and a new interest in colorful ornamental trop-ical fish also contributed to the goldfish's decline in popularity. "Plump" goldfish could not compete with those swimming jewels, the warm-water tropical fish. Technical innovations changed the nature of the aquarium hobby. The popular new varieties of tropical fish required heaters, aerators, and filters, without which goldfish did very well. Because of their ease of care, goldfish were more or less the precursors of the tropical fish hobby.

Goldfish development in the Far East, however, did not slow down. The tropical fish hobby never completely replaced the goldfish hobby in China and Japan, where goldfish, after all, had

Goldfish hatchery in Peking

11

Goldfish in a Chinese ceramic tub.

a headstart of some 900 years. The rising number of aquarium hobbyists provided new impetus for Far Eastern fish breeders, with the result that competition between the three main types of hobby fish breeding, i.e., goldfish, ornamental carp, and tropical fish, produced new forms of goldfish and encouraged their proliferation. The domestic goldfish, derived from the gray wild goldfish, and the colorful ornamental carp or koi, bred from the grayish-brown common carp, competed successfully in popularity with the plethora of tropical fish varieties.

Modern goldfish cultivators have created a great number of varieties and forms. Without a doubt, we can say that Chinese and Japanese breeders have completely modernized goldfish. In addition to the classic veiltails, the most diverse body and head shapes imaginable have been bred, not to mention bodies and fins of all colors—gold, dark red, variegated (calico), bright red,

black, and white, to name but a few. The emphasis on fragility and silkiness of the fins, once so common, has been replaced by an emphasis on diversification and variety in shape and color. The incredible development in this area over the past few decades is an indication of the continuing advances in goldfish breeding. It took a long time for those new and beautiful goldfish varieties finally to reach the western world.

GOLDFISH AND THEIR NEW POPULARITY

"Ugh, goldfish!" That's the reaction of some of the more scientifically-oriented aquarium hobbyists whenever goldfish are mentioned. "They are boring." "I don't want them in my aquarium because they stir up the bottom." "They

Introduction

Selecting young fish in a Peking fish hatchery.

are so easy to care for that keeping them is no challenge." "They won't breed in my tank." These are the kinds of comments often heard when goldfish are mentioned to experienced fish hobbyists. But didn't most of us as aquarists pass similar judgment on goldfish when we were seeking trophies and dreamt of breeding so-called "problem fish" like neon tetras or the *Rasbora* varieties? Goldfish were, after all, synonymous with distorted glass bowls, or with placid fish in largely neglected, algae-filled aquariums or tubs at the pet shop—a symbol of unprofessional aquarium science.

Whenever we think back to our beginnings as aquarists, we have to admit that it was a shame to dismiss goldfish so completely and so unjustly disdainfully. Goldfish would have been a better, and easier, starting point than the expensive delicate tropical fish with which many of us started our hobby.

In the late 1950s, several aquarium journal articles about goldfish attracted our attention. The articles described goldfish from the Far East with shapes and colors unknown to us. We read of the export of considerable numbers of fish from China and Japan. We learned that goldfish breeding was on an upward swing and that, because of the great demand, the various forms were no longer bred and kept in cement tubs and basins, but rather in breeding ponds and tanks, imitating the new Japanese practice. We were fascinated, and decided, then and there, that we, too, would become involved with goldfish. By a stroke of luck, a trip to China coincided with this decision.

We spent most of our free time in China in search of goldfish. We visited breeding establishments, attended the breeding exhibition in front of Peking's open air market, and visited the hatcheries famous for the best breeding stocks.

In Peking, we realized that goldfish breeders were able to breed their animals according to just about any whim. We were also convinced that goldfish can and have been domesticated as much as any four-legged pet; so much so that they probably could not survive in the natural environment of their recent ancestors. Our third realization was that goldfish are undemanding, easy to keep and care for, and require very little time from their owner, important features in an animal kept only out of affection, as a hobby, a pet. Our Chinese colleagues also taught us that goldfish should be observed from above, not from the side through a wall of glass. This feature stems from the fact that when the original forms were developed more than a thousand years ago, there were no glass bowls. Our fifth lesson was that goldfish are very tame and may be very easily trained.

We also learned many details of the art of keeping, breeding, and selecting goldfish, about Chinese goldfish culture, and about the devotion to goldfish as symbols of fertility shown by people in the Far East. We were also able to bring home several hundred young goldfish.

WHAT GOLDFISH CAN OFFER US

Many people like to keep domesticated plants and animals in their homes. Goldfish provide a novel source of color and add to the attractiveness of the decor. A goldfish aquarium can be just as attractive in a group of house plants in front of a bay window as in a wall of bookshelves. The great variety of goldfish bowls and aquariums reflects their decorative uses. More important, however, is that these containers provide sufficient freedom of movement for the goldfish that are to live in them.

Outdoors, goldfish can enhance the beauty of a garden in small ornamental ponds. Here, goldfish appear as flashes of constantly moving color, because they usually do not hide in the vegetation, as so many of our native pond fish tend to do. For this reason goldfish are often thought of as the "flowers" among fish—being as conspicuous and striking as are garden flowers in a background of greenery.

The apparent increased interest in goldfish has resulted in the establishment of a number of large goldfish hatcheries, both here and in the Far East. These hatcheries consist of different pools for fry, for young fish, and for breeding stock, and separate pools for overwintering. These pools are equipped with elaborate filtering systems that circulate and clean the large volumes of water required to raise the many thousands of goldfish each produces.

Artificial insemination is a commonly used method for goldfish reproduction in these large hatchery operations. Over the years these techniques have been nearly perfected and produce a much higher yield of fertilized eggs and viable fry than do natural breeding methods.

HISTORY OF GOLDFISH

A THOUSAND-YEAR HISTORY IN CHINA

There are numerous legends in various Asian cultures concerning the origins of goldfish. Z. Kászoni (*Aquariums,* 1972) mentions four of them.

According to one legend, the Chinese province of Shen-Si suffered from a terrible, prolonged drought during the reign of Emperor Ping-Wang. The starving people prayed to their gods to dispel the drought. The gods took pity on them, and soon ample rain drenched the countryside and springs gushed from the rocks. The goldfish appeared with the water as a gift from the gods to suffering mankind.

Another legend has goldfish originating in the heavens, where the nimble fish played among the clouds. But they were careless, and tumbled down to earth.

According to a third legend, a violent storm stirred up the ocean down to its deepest depths. It tossed the goldfish up from the bottom of the

Wooden goldfish—an example of Chinese craftsmanship

sea; by chance, they fell into the sacred lake at Tsche-Tschian where they were discovered by Chinese fishermen.

The final legend recounts the story of a very lovely girl, even more beautiful than the dawn. She was in love with a young lad, who left her. The girl cried bitterly for her unfaithful lover. Her tears, falling to earth like pearls, awakened the beautiful goldfish to life.

These legends attest to the popularity of goldfish. There are no reliable accounts of the initial appearance of goldfish, however. The beginnings of goldfish breeding can be traced back a thousand years, although a few original drawings from the third to fifth centuries already show red-scaled fish in decorative ponds. There are even earlier references to goldfish, some of them almost 2500 years old. The song collection by Si-King, dating from the 6th century A.D., contains lyrics about goldfish in connection with the construction of the imperial palace.

Between 968 and 975 A.D., several goldfish hatcheries were founded in Kiahsing, in southern China, at nearly the same time. A little later, other hatcheries appeared at the Luho Pagoda in Hang-Chow, and in Nanking. Goldfish were already protected in these places, the consumption of "red fish" being strictly forbidden. The fish were still kept in a feral state—that is, they lived in large lakes overgrown with abundant vegetation, a condition reflecting the original natural environment of goldfish. For that reason, there was no control over populations or breeding. Varieties having different shapes and colors were as yet unknown. The domestication of goldfish is regarded as having begun during the Sung Dynasty (960–1279 A.D.).

In 1163 A.D., Emperor Hiau-Tsung and his court started to raise goldfish for the sole purpose of His Majesty's entertainment and pleasure. This period is the real beginning of goldfish breeding, since the fish were cared for and systematically bred by trained experts. The first color variations appeared: golden-yellow, silvery white, and black and white. Following the death of Emperor Hiau-Tsung goldfish became popular throughout China. Poets and historians immortalized that "wonderful being," the goldfish, in numerous literary works.

Between 1279 and 1546 A.D., keeping and breeding goldfish spread to all levels of society and was no longer a pastime for a few rich people. After 1330 A.D., during the Yuan Dynasty, goldfish were introduced into the cooler northern parts of China, including Peking. After 1510 A.D., numerous small ponds and tubs containing goldfish could be found outside the walls of the Forbidden City. During this time even the poorer people began to get involved with goldfish. Lacking the money to build ponds, they kept their new pets in a variety of fired-clay pots.

According to historical sources, there was hardly a dwelling or garden without goldfish during the reign of the Ming Dynasty (1368–1644); breeding was practiced throughout the country. However, the results of observations and investigations of the fish, as well as the methods of their care and breeding, were kept strictly secret everywhere. During this time systematic breeding, requiring a great deal of expertise, produced goldfish varieties which featured transparent scales, colorful, thickset bodies, and protruding eyes.

Before the middle of the seventeenth century, most colors and shapes of goldfish known today had already been created. Later efforts resulted only in additional combinations or a more pronounced expression of existing characteristics. It is obvious that the varieties that originated during this period reveal their full splendor when viewed from above, rather than from the side. This, as we have learned, is because glass, our customary aquarium material, was totally unknown in China at the time (it was invented in Byzantium). Consequently, breeding concentrated mainly on goldfish which look beautiful in their bronze, ceramic, or wooden containers.

Starting in the 17th century, goldfish appear

in literature quite frequently. But all authors are guilty of the same "omission": the method of producing different varieties is never once discussed. Breeding and selection techniques were shrouded in a mystical fog and were handed down verbally from father to son. They remained the secret of goldfish-breeding families—and they were as precious as gold.

Toward the end of the Ching Dynasty, between 1848 and 1925, several additional goldfish varieties resulted from planned interbreeding and deliberate selection. They included the black telescope eye, the lionhead, the celestial, the pearl scale, and the bubble eye.

EXPORTS TO OTHER COUNTRIES

During the Middle Ages, the Chinese even exported their goldfish. We can find several references to goldfish exports to Japan, although the Japanese are unable to give any precise dates. Some researchers believe that the fish were first imported to Japan in 1502, while the years 1616 and 1619 are cited by others. Japanese goldfish breeders made so much progress during the 18th, 19th, and 20th centuries that they became serious competitors of the Chinese. Today the Japanese easily command the lead in the goldfish trade with an annual export of many millions of goldfish to all corners of the world. Korea and Singapore have also achieved high production levels in goldfish breeding, although less than those of China and Japan.

In 1691 the first goldfish arrived in England, where keeping goldfish became a fad overnight. Later, the fish spread to France, Portugal, Spain, and Italy. The first breeding success on the European continent was recorded in the Netherlands in 1780. In Germany, goldfish keeping and breeding reached its zenith in the 1870s.

Louis XIV of France made a gift of goldfish imported from China to Madame de Pompadour, and the Russian Prince Potemkin loved goldfish so much that he decorated the tables of

Decorative goldfish pattern in a Japanese drawing

his famous banquets with living goldfish kept in glass globes.

The first goldfish arrived in America in 1850, probably from Japanese sources. Goldfish were a big sensation in New York department stores in 1865.

GOLDFISH IN ART

Goldfish play an important role in art, especially Oriental art. They appear on porcelain, ceramic, and iron dishes, are depicted on textiles and in woodcuts, used in decorative architectural elements, and portrayed in paintings and small sculptures. China has even produced a goldfish stamp series. In modern Japanese art, small goldfish sculptures demonstrate the continuing interest in the subject. Even the American motion picture industry has immortalized the goldfish in the role of Cleo in the Walt Disney production of "Pinocchio."

At the turn of the century, goldfish kept in glass bowls were a common and very popular decorative element in homes. During World War I, interest in keeping goldfish waned considerably, however, and during the 1920s, goldfish were replaced by tropical fish from South America, Africa, and Southeast Asia. It was no longer fashionable to keep goldfish, and goldfish hobbyists were looked down upon by other fish hobbyists. Today, goldfish are enjoying a renaissance because of their diversity of shapes and colors and because of the minimal care they require.

GOLDFISH BIOLOGY

CLASSIFICATION

The wild ancestor of the domestic goldfish is the carp species *Carassius auratus gibelio* Bloch (1783).

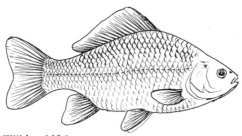

Wild goldfish

The genus *Carassius* belongs to the carp family (Cyprinidae), which is classified in the suborder of carplike fish (Cyprinoidei) in the order of cyprinid fish (Cypriniformes) in the superorder of bony fishes (Teleostei).

The goldfish species is closely related to the crucian carp (*Carassius carassius*) Linnaeus (1758).

ANATOMY

Wild goldfish are 12 to 16 inches (30 to 40 centimeters) long, excluding the caudal, or tail, fins; they very rarely attain a length of 18 inches (45 centimeters). Their weight ranges from ½ to 2¼ pounds (0.2 to 1.0 kilograms). The body form is elongated and laterally compressed.

The dorsal (back) color of wild goldfish is olive-green; the sides are silvery, often tinged with yellow. The ventrium, or abdominal region, is yellow-green, and the fins are silver-gray.

Goldfish have four pharyngeal teeth on each of the bilateral pharyngeal bones and 39 to 50 gill rakers.

The goldfish's lateral line (*linea lateralis*) has from 28 to 33 perforated scales, with 5 to 7 rows of scales arranged above and below the lateral line. The scales of wild goldfish are considerably larger than those of crucian carp.

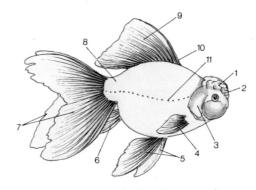

Goldfish parts as exemplified by the parts of an oranda: 1) cap, 2) nasal appendage (narial bouquet), 3) gill flap or cover (operculum), 4) pectoral fin, 5) ventral or pelvic fin, 6) anal fin, 7) caudal or tail fin, 8) tail base (peduncle), 9) dorsal or back fin, 10) hard ray, 11) lateral line

The goldfish fin arrangement is D III-IV /14/ 15-19, A II-III 5-6, P I/15/16/17, and V I 8, where D is the symbol for dorsal or back fins, A for the anal fin located under the caudal or tail fins, P for the pectoral or breast fins, and V for the ventral or pelvic fins. The Roman numerals indicate the unbranched, hard fin rays while the Arabic numerals indicate the number of forked, soft fin rays.

Both wild and domesticated goldfish have 94 diploid chromosomes (47 haploid). By contrast,

Goldfish

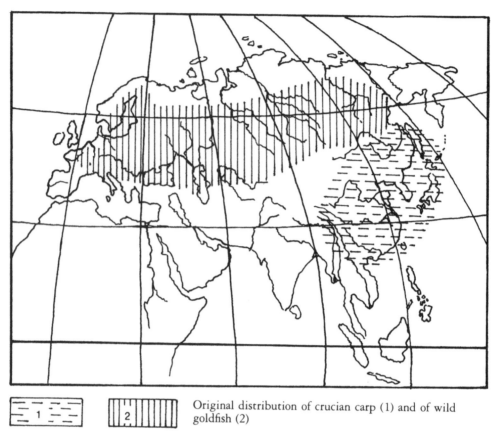

Original distribution of crucian carp (1) and of wild goldfish (2)

the common ornamental carp has 104 diploid chromosomes (52 haploid).

DISTRIBUTION AND FEEDING HABITS

Since prehistoric times crucian carp have lived over most of Europe, except parts of Scandinavia and the Iberian peninsula, and in Central Asia as far east as the Lena River. Wild goldfish are found in Asia from the Amur River to northeastern India. In the past few years they have been introduced to all of India, Europe, and North America.

Wild goldfish live in marshes, swamps, lakes, and river backwaters, partly because their oxy-gen requirement is quite modest. They eat mostly insect larvae (e.g. *Chironomus*), zooplankton (e.g. *Daphnia, Cyclops, Bosmina, Chydorus*), and mud-dwelling worms (*Tubifex*). They also consume large amounts of aquatic plants (sphagnum moss, filamentous algae, pondweed and pondweed seeds).

LIFE CYCLE

Reproductive maturity is reached between the second and third year. Goldfish have some particularly noteworthy reproductive characteristics. For example, a two-year-old male (buck) is transformed into a female (roe). The eggs, laid in quantities of 150,000 to 300,000 per fish, can be fertilized by males of other carp species (a process called gynogenesis). The sperm of the other species do not unite with the eggs of the female, but serve only to stimulate their growth and development. This form of reproduction, technically called "parthenogenesis," is also known as "maiden" or "virginal birth."

Normally, a goldfish's life begins with fertilization of the egg, when it is referred to as an embryo. The embryonic stage then continues until hatching time.

Hatched fish that cannot yet make use of bodily orifices are called larvae. This phase lasts until the onset of actual external feeding. Larvae absorb oxygen through their skin and are nourished by the yolk sac. As soon as they first ingest food through the mouth, they are designated *fry* or *fingerlings*. They remain fry until they start consuming their adult diet of *Daphnia*, insect larvae, *Tubifex* worms, and other items. At the end of their first summer, the young fry are called *yearlings*.

Newly hatched fry of domestic goldfish are approximately 3/16" (6 mm) long. Given a proper diet and adequate care, a fish will reach a length of 1/2"–5/8" (12 mm–15 mm) after two weeks. At one month, goldfish normally measure 3/4" (2 cm), at two months 1½" (4 cm), and at five months 2½"–2¾" (6 cm–7 cm). The fish are fully grown at the end of the third summer.

Domestic goldfish have an average life expectancy of 7 to 8 years, but a few individuals have lived to the grand old age of 20–28 years.

VARIATIONS IN THE WILD

The wild goldfish populations of southeast Asia have always produced a few individuals with distinctly golden or orange pigmentation. For unknown reasons the yellow chromatic cells (xanthophores) in the skin multiply abnormally, conferring their unique color to the entire fish.

In fact, our first shipment of 50,000 fish from Peking, for distribution in Hungary, contained several such orange-colored goldfish.

Similarly, common carp (*Cyprinus carpio*), tench (*Tinca tinca*), and a few other species occasionally produce bright goldfish instead of the customary silver-gray ones. However, "golden carp" should not be confused with the domestic goldfish because the latter is derived from a different species. The Japanese have bred numerous varieties from golden carp (i.e. red, black, orange, and spotted forms, to name just a few), for ornamental purposes. These ornamentals which weigh 1–1¾ lb., are called "koi" in the Land of the Rising Sun.

VARIATIONS IN DOMESTIC GOLDFISH

The domestic goldfish, *Carassius auratus auratus* Linnaeus (1758), was bred in China from the orange variant of the wild goldfish, *Carassius auratus gibelio,* more than a thousand years ago. The major characteristics distinguishing the present-day domestic goldfish from the wild form are:

1. shorter and rounder bodies,
2. the dorsal and caudal fins of several varieties have become enlarged "veils" and more delicate,
3. in some of the highly-prized varieties, dorsal fins have disappeared altogether.
4. epidermis and cuticle skin layers on the heads of several varieties have become thicker; the increased cell growth has resulted in the creation of "lionheads," "caps," "hoods," and so forth.
5. the eyes in certain varieties protrude abnormally, resembling "telescopes."
6. in many varieties, typical scale iridescence has yielded to colors such as red, black, white, or calico (multicolored).

In each goldfish variety one or more of these characteristic features combine to give a unique, unmistakable appearance to that variety. This makes individual fish not showing the characteristic markings for a given variety easy to spot.

Color and Scales

Japanese fish journals have featured several articles on special methods used for influencing a fish's color—to alter the color determined by heredity. According to these articles, scraping off part of the fish's skin with a sharp razor blade removes a portion of the black pigment cells. This, in turn, leads to changes in coloration. The juice from a certain flower containing compounds similar to oxalic acid also alters a fish's color. Some breeders apply a mixture of alum and prunes to their fish to effect color changes. According to another source, color changes result if some of the dorsal scales are carefully scraped off, followed by an application of glacial acetic acid, rubbing alcohol, salicylic acid, carbonic acid, and diluted hydrochloric acid. This treatment causes minor destruction of chromatic cells, resulting in color changes in 2- to 3-month-old fish that have already started to revert to the wild-type green coloration or have begun to fade to white or orange shades. Japanese breeders recommend using these methods repeatedly in order to obtain optimum results. We have not tested any of these processes ourselves and thus cannot judge their effectiveness.

Genetically, goldfish may be unicolor (golden yellow, lemon yellow, orange, red, white, black, lavender, or brown) or calico (various combinations of the above colors). There have been reports that if a goldfish should become blind, its body color will turn dark, even black.

We distinguish between two major categories of scale types:
a) natural scales which maintain original wildtype characteristics,
b) transparent or semi-transparent (including reticulated, mosaic, and serial scale arrangements).

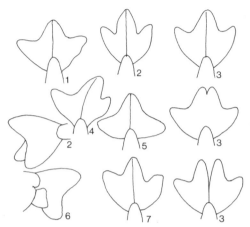

The most frequent shapes of paired (divided) caudal fins (after Matsui): 1, 2, 4, 5, 6, 7, = irregular; 3 = regular caudal fin shapes.

Fins

The shape, size, position, and transparency of the fins, in particular the caudal fin, constitute major distinguishing characteristics of some goldfish varieties.

The caudal fin may be single—identical in shape to that of the wild goldfish. This is termed "homocercal," and consists of virtually symmetrical upper and lower lobes. In addition there are double and, possibly, even triple, and quadruple fins, fins with inverted "Y" and "V" shapes, and, finally, the so-called "peacock" caudal fins, or "ribbon tails."

The length of certain fins is also variable—the lengthening of dorsal and caudal fins creates "veils."

In some varieties, such as the highly-prized lionheads, the most distinctive characteristic is the complete absence of the dorsal fin and the smoothly contoured, convex shape of the back.

Goldfish with divided and veillike caudal fins and anal fins, and with oval body shapes develop considerably slower than fish with simple fins and normal, or nearly normal, anatomy. For that reason, they must always be kept separate when breeding.

GOLDFISH BEHAVIOR

DIRECTION, BALANCE, AND PERCEPTION

Sensory organs play as important a role in the lives of aquatic animals, including fish, as in the lives of terrestrial species. Water is a medium in direct contact with the bodies of fish and thus influences all their vital functions. Any changes in the aqueous environment are perceived by the fish's sensory organs. The number and complexity of behavioral patterns of any one fish species increases as the brain and sensory organs of that species become larger and more complex.

Among the many goldfish varieties there are those whose skull bones are covered with a thick caplike epidermal growth of the kind seen in orandas or lionheads. In some cases this feature grows outward as well as inward, causing the delicate ear labyrinth, a most important organ for the sense of balance, to be subjected to ever-greater pressure. The increase in pressure is accompanied by a corresponding increase in abnormal body movements or "posture," and the fish's movements are more and more altered in an uncharacteristic way.

Sound vibrations are picked up by the swim bladder via the skin and muscles, and are then conducted to the inner ear. This is, essentially, how the fish hear.

A faint line, the "lateral line," runs along the middle of each side of the fish. That line is an extremely important organ because it governs the fish's perception of water currents, of the directional movement of a school of fish, and of certain sound waves. The ability of fish to swim against the current is also due to the lateral line.

It is thus the organ largely responsible for triggering the evasive behavior of fish—that is, their reaction to any change, disturbance or stress.

RESPONSE TO STRESS

Evasive behavior patterns are of two types, namely inherent and acquired. Almost all fish species will react to a dark shape swimming on the surface by flight, for instance. In a hatchery pond, on the other hand, the carp become accustomed to the boat that brings them their food. To them, the boat's shadow and noise become synonymous with food, and they follow the boat instead of taking flight.

As soon as a fish perceives any danger in a particular situation, it flees, mustering its entire muscular resources to do so. The flight attempts can involve "running" in open water without changing depth (whitefish), running to the bottom (carp), or running to the bank or shore. Carp living in hatchery ponds occasionally react in very unusual ways when they are suddenly disturbed. As an example, workers in a certain fish hatchery preparing to harvest yearling carp drained most of the water from the pond. Tens of thousands of fish were gathered in the long channels at the bottom when helicopters arrived and generated high waves as they passed low over the water. The small carp crowded together in the channels were so disoriented by the noise and the waves that, in a matter of seconds, they retreated to the muddy channel banks and burrowed right into the ground. Catching them was well-nigh impossible after that. A similar phenomenon was observed in a frozen fish pond which a group of children used as an ice skating rink. Carp overwintering in the deepest part of the pond were roused after a short time by the commotion above them and became increasingly restless. Ultimately, they tried to seek protection in the reeds of the shallow bank areas, where a few days later they were found, frozen to death.

Such behavior patterns have been observed in fish overwintering in natural lakes and rivers. For example, at the end of winter, when the ice covering the Danube River, in Hungary, breaks up with mighty cracking sounds and starts to drift, the terrified fish begin to flee. The majority of them rush to the river banks—where the ice is breaking and drifting away first. In Lake Balaton, the fish act in just the opposite way. The storm-driven waves of the lake break apart the thick ice layer with deafening explosions and force great chunks toward the shore. The fish that usually overwinter near shore escape toward the center of the lake.

FEEDING BEHAVIOR

Researchers interested in fish biology and biochemistry have learned in the course of detailed studies that a center within the brain responsible for the sensations of hunger and satiation governs the fish's search for food in a way similar to that of more advanced vertebrates. This brain center probably reacts to reduced concentrations of nutrients (sugars, fats) in the blood. The sensation of hunger thus originates in the brain and moves the fish to search for (forage) and consume food.

In fish, this stimulus is significantly influenced by the temperature of the water, unlike animals with constant body temperatures. Therefore, the biological activity of fish, as animals with a variable body temperature (poikilothermic or cold-blooded) depends essentially on the temperature of their environment. This fundamental principle is thus one of the prime considerations in a determination of how much fish will eat.

In addition to the internal stimulus of hunger, foraging activity also depends on the general state of the fish's nutrition and health. A thin but healthy individual kept without food for awhile forages more actively, even under adverse conditions. This behavior continues until the fish is in good shape. Every fish hobbyist has probably observed fish gasping for air at the water surface after feeding. This phenomenon is not a sign of any abnormal health condition, but simply demonstrates that a full fish needs more oxygen than a hungry one. There is a definite connection between food consumption and the oxygen content of the water.

Members of the carp family do not have stomachs, and therefore feed more or less continuously. Therefore, it is recommended that carp raised in fish ponds be fed twice daily during the warm summer months—in the early morning and in the early afternoon. Naturally, the condition of being "full" depends on the general condition of the fish. Even when they are hungry, their state of health and body size, and the water temperature remain determining factors.

The Search for Food
Searching for food is the first or "appetitive" behavior in the pattern of the feeding process. As we have already indicated, this searching pattern is induced by a sensation of hunger. Every living being, including a fish, commences the search for food as a result of this internal stimulus. Fish orient their search first of all on the question of whether they can engage in searching for food without danger. Carp then simply change from a state of rest to active movement and, after a little "stretching," begin foraging. However, the behavior is not invari-

TOP: The common domestic goldfish, basic form.
BOTTOM LEFT: Some color variations of the common domestic goldfish
BOTTOM RIGHT: Normal veiltail, commercial variety

able; individuals show great differences even in the initial phase. Some of the carp in fish ponds swim to the feeding site first to consume the food provided for them until they are full. Only then will they embark on a "gourmet tour" to hunt aquatic animals (plankton, snails, insect larvae). Other carp reverse the pattern: they conclude their early morning food search with the food set out for them. And then, there are solitary foragers as well as fish that feed in groups.

Fish feeding on the bottom often ingest large quantities of mud and sand along with their food. Edible substances are sorted out in their mouths; food is retained, unpalatable items are spit out. The fish may also expel everything in their mouths again because they cannot properly separate food from detrites. But they do not give up so easily; they usually renew their search for the discarded morsels and ingest them again. Generally, the longitudinal axis of bottom-feeding carp forms an acute angle with the water surface. But when the fish are burrowing for food deep down in the mud, they often stand vertically, trying to penetrate the muddy or sandy bottom by powerful strokes of their tails.

When carp are fed with automatic feeding machines, the fish need only a few days to learn that their food supply depends on their hitting the tab or dispensing lever, and they operate the dispenser as their appetites dictate. Automatic feeding devices have proven to be invaluable in large-scale carp cultivation. The method saves large amounts of food and avoids excessive, damaging overfeeding. More and more fish hatcheries have been installing these feeders for their carp.

The topic of food raises the question of choice.

To what extent do fish select their food? We believe that they are essentially like us—that is, that each fish has a preference. This preferred food, when available, becomes its main food supply; in addition, the fish continuously consumes secondary food sources, including special types with limited availability (location or season). However, if fish are very hungry, they are—except for a certain few varieties—not choosy about their diet.

Food Consumption

The consumption or actual ingestion of food searched for and found is the second or "consummative" phase of the feeding process.

The consummative phase is generally characterized by more uniform behavior patterns than the individual feeding habits displayed in the appetitive phase. The patterns are largely inherited, rather than learned, and are thus characteristic for each species. Simply put: All fish of a given species consume food in the same manner. The chopping, grinding, mastication of food into small bits is characteristic of fish belonging to the carp family. Chewing does not take place in the mouth cavity but in the pharynx by means of pharyngeal teeth. Regularly shaped teeth formed by an extension of the gill arch and coated with enamel are located on the pharyngeal bones. By the shape and number of these teeth you can deduce the diet of a fish.

WANDERING AND MIGRATION

Fish movements are of two major types: wandering and migrating. Wandering is short-distance, frequent and random-appearing changes of locale resulting from the search for food, for new hiding places, or for spawning sites.

Migration consists of long-distance movements connected with major life cycle events—spawning, movements to and from nursery areas, or seasonal changes in geographical distribution.

TOP: The rare eggfish, or maruko (brass colored), a variety which, like the lionhead, lacks the dorsal fin.
BOTTOM LEFT: Lionhead
BOTTOM RIGHT: Young redcaps, a variety derived from the oranda.

Goldfish

MATING BEHAVIOR

There are detailed studies of the spawning of carp in the wild. Males arrive much earlier at the spawning site, which is located in calm waters overgrown with grass or pond-weed. They begin looking for the females, swimming back and forth in visible excitement and lacking their usual caution. In the morning they perform the characteristic spawning ritual even in the absence of the females. They drive one another, spout water at the surface, and often raise their backs out of the water. In the presence of females the males, as if reacting to some kind of signal, begin circling faster. The area being used becomes smaller and smaller. A few individuals struggle along in only inches of water, almost lying on their sides in their efforts to surmount obstacles. Their bodies may even jut halfway out of the water.

It is the goal of these fish to secure the most advantageous position near the females. Then one or two, later five or six, males start chasing a ripe female. Males typically stiffen and collapse their dorsal fins now, again and again. They rub against the females in the water and poke the abdominal region of the females with their heads, thereby stimulating them to discharge their roe. The shallow water is roiled by fins thrashing in the water, until, finally, each female releases her roe. The roe jetting out is fertilized by the cloud of milt released by the males. The outer layer of the eggs becomes sticky when it contacts the water, and the spawn sticks like small pearls to the grass blades. If fertilization is successful, the spawn continues to develop in the small, transparent balls; if not, the eggs become cloudy and burst apart sooner or later.

VARIETIES OF GOLDFISH

There are far more known goldfish races, varieties, forms, and types than are described in the following section. We have purposely limited ourselves to the more important, internationally well-known varieties. Forms locally common in China, Japan, or Korea often do not appear in this country. Therefore, describing them in this book would be of little help to the goldfish hobbyist in the United States.

Wildtype Orange Goldfish
(Also called Common Wild Goldfish; Japanese: Hibuna)

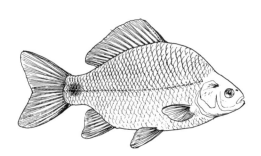

This is the orange variety of the wildtype goldfish, and as such it is the oldest and most common variety. In shape, size, scale arrangement, and fin number and structure, the wildtype orange form is identical to the normal wildtype. Only its color, ranging from golden-yellow to orange to dark red, distinguishes it from its ancestor.

Wildtype orange goldfish occur in natural bodies of water throughout Southeast Asia, and also appear as "throwbacks" among the offspring of other goldfish breeds. The variety is available all over the world.

Common Domestic Goldfish
(Japanese: Wakin)

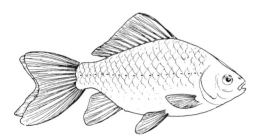

The common domestic goldfish is the classic goldfish derived from the wildtype orange goldfish of ancient China. The other goldfish varieties were created from this form by selective breeding and crossbreeding.

The fish still closely resembles its ancestors, but its body is significantly more thickset and stocky. In some varieties, the caudal fins are divided (paired). Popular colors include bright orange-red and calico, as the varieties spotted white and orange-red are usually called.

Common domestic goldfish are easy to keep and relatively robust. They are relatively insensitive to cold, being capable of living even under ice. They may thus be kept in outdoor ponds all year round. This very common variety is found throughout the world.

Comet
(Japanese: Tetsugyo)

The comet's appearance is reminiscent of the common goldfish but differs considerably from that variety in having much longer fins. The caudal fin is single (undivided). Body color is

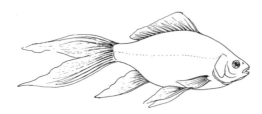

usually orange-red or spotted with white, and the fins are transparent.

The fish is easy to take care of, inexpensive, and found throughout the world.

Veiltail
(Also called Ribbontail, Fantail, Fringetail, or Twintail, depending on fin length and form; Japanese: Ryukin)

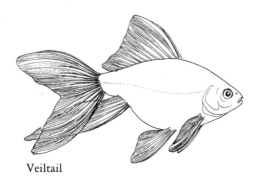

Veiltail

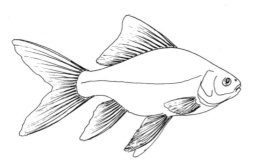

Hybrid between a wild goldfish and a veiltail.

As its name indicates, this variety's paired caudal fin extends into a veil hanging perpendicularly from the body. The caudal fin is always

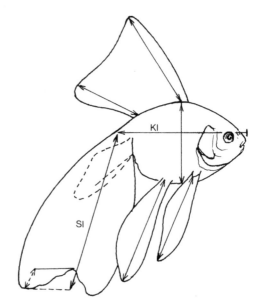

Body/fin ratio of the veiltail: BL = body length; TL = tail length

longer than the fish's body (minimum ratio of 5:4). The veil form is characteristic of the remaining finnage, as well. Fin length determines the value of individual fish. Veiltail goldfish may be orange, red, black, or calico.

They may be kept in aquariums or ornamental ponds. Water temperatures below 37°F (3°C) damage the delicate fins. The variety is found throughout the world.

Egg Fish
(Japanese: Maruko)

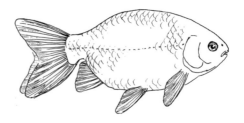

The maruko is one of the oldest varieties of goldfish originally bred in China and later imported to Japan. It is the ancestor of the famous lionhead goldfish.

Its predominant feature is its stocky, oval body and its dark red color. All fins are short, the caudal fin is paired, and the dorsal fin absent.

As a variety in its own right, the maruko is nearly extinct, but it may appear as an occasional breeding "throwback." Limited numbers of this type are still bred in China, Japan, and Korea.

Lionhead
(Also called Bramblehead; Japanese: Ranchu)

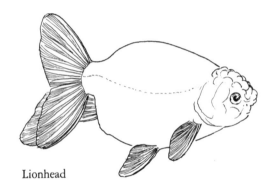

Lionhead

This oddly-shaped fish originated in China.

The fish has a thickset body reminiscent of a chicken egg. The top and sides of its head have bright red, tumorlike growths that resemble a lion's mane, hence the name. The wide, convex back has no fins. A short, paired caudal fin arises from the large, well-developed base (peduncle) of the tail. Relatively large scales cover the entire body. The body and fins are dark orange. If the curve of the back is humped or not totally symmetrical, or if there is a vestigial dorsal fin, the fish is considered flawed and should be excluded from breeding.

Lionheads prefer warm water. During the summer the temperature of their water should be 64°–77°F (18°–25°C), and winter water temperatures should be 57°–61°F (14°–16°C). The lionhead is a rare and highly-prized fish. Individual lionheads in the United States have cost

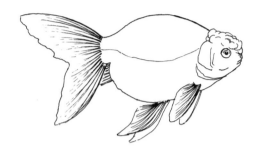

Hybrid between a lionhead and an oranda

as much as $1000. In Japan this variety is crowned "King of the Goldfish," and people organize special competitions and exhibitions just for lionheads. Lionheads are also very popular in China and Singapore, but there are relatively few in Europe and the United States.

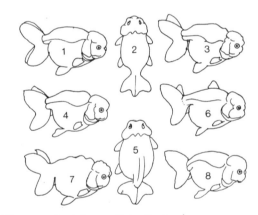

Different varietal forms of the lionhead
1 = ideal body shape
2–8 = flawed body shapes

Lionhead of Osaka
(Japanese: Osaka Ranchu)

This pleasing Japanese variety was bred from the unicolor dark red egg fish (maruko). Its body is thickset and egg-shaped. It has no dorsal fin, and the caudal fin is relatively short and fan-shaped. As a result, this variety tips and sways from side to side as it swims. These lionheads do not have the full "lion's mane" hood—only

31

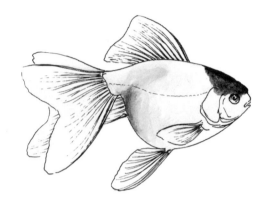

the upper portion of the head is covered by a patch of thicker skin. Head and fins are red while the rest of the body is covered with large white and red blotches.

The Lionhead of Osaka is a very rare form nearly extinct.

White Egg Fish
(Japanese: Nankin)

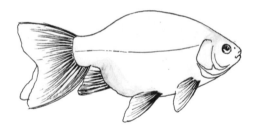

As the name implies, the ancestor of this variety, developed in Japan, is the egg fish or maruko.

The relatively large, robust body of this variety is egg-shaped. The fish has normal, non-protruding eyes. Its caudal peduncle is somewhat elongated, its caudal fin is paired, and there is no dorsal fin. The fish's body is white, often with spots of varying sizes, and the fins may be bright yellow or pink.

The rare Nankin is kept predominantly in Japan, where it is bred exclusively in the Izumo District.

Redhead

This goldfish, with is spectacular features, originated in China. Its medium-sized body is somewhat cylindrical in shape. Its caudal fin is paired and slightly veiled. Its most prominent characteristic is its bright yellow color—body as well as fins—and the presence of a bright red cap on the forehead, extending down to the eyeline.

Redheads are very rare and interesting fish. They look particularly attractive in a light blue bowl. Common in China, Hong Kong, and Singapore, this variety is represented in Europe and North America only by a few specimens.

Calico
(Usually called Calico Telescope Eye, or Dragon Eye)

The calico is an attractive spotted variety, originally from China. The caudal fin of this goldfish variety is paired and veillike. Head and body are both spotted, i.e., calico, in white, yellow, orange-red, brown and black, and the bright yellow fins are usually graced with small brown dots. The calico's eyes protrude approximately ⁵⁄₁₆ to ³⁄₈ inch (8–10 millimeters) to form the so-called telescope eyes. The small protruding corneal region in front of the eyeballs is extraordinarily sensitive. Great care is thus required to prevent injury to the eyes, particularly when netting the fish to take it out of the water. The unusual size of the eyes, especially in fingerlings, has another disadvantage. Other species delight in nipping at the eyes, which can lead to blindness. For that reason calicos should be kept and raised in separate containers.

Individuals of this variety give a particularly unique effect in a bowl with a white or black bottom. Calicos are comparatively common and are found throughout the world.

Red Telescope Eye
(Also called Globe-Eye; Japanese: Demenkin)

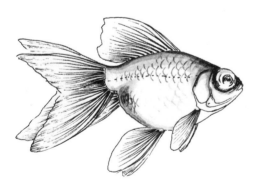

The terms used to describe the calico also apply to the red telescope eye, which is also Chinese in origin. The one basic difference is that red telescope eyes are completely red.

Red telescope eyes look very pretty in white or black bowls, and the variety is hardy enough to be kept in outdoor ponds. Red telescope eyes are quite common all over the world and are very easy to care for.

Black Moor
(Also called Black Telescope Eye; Japanese: Kuro Demenkin)

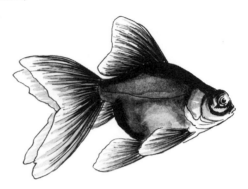

The black moor is an extremely interesting and unique goldfish variety from China. It differs only in color from the red telescope eye described above.

This variety's striking black coloration, with its velvety sheen, is caused by an unusually large number of black pigment cells in the skin.

Extreme care is necessary not to injure the massive, protruding eyes and the transparent corneas, especially when netting the fish. Young fish cannot be kept with other types of goldfish because the developing eyes will be bitten off. The black moor is very susceptible to velvet disease (costiasis).

This fish prefers warm water temperatures and cannot winter outdoors. Black moors look good in white, yellow, or light red bowls. The variety is moderately priced and popular all over the world.

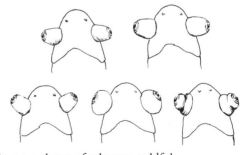

Various eye shapes of telescope goldfish

Pearlscale
(Japanese: Chunshuyui)

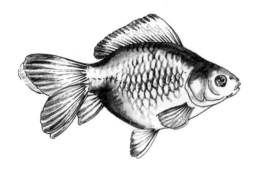

Pearlscales have thickset, stocky bodies. Laterally, especially in the front half of the body above and below the lateral line, the pearly center of each scale protrudes slightly in the shape of a rice grain. The total effect is one of small pearls or rice grains pasted to the fish's body. The pearlscale's caudal fin is paired; dorsal, ventral, and pectoral fins have a slight veil form. The fish's body is normally bright red; some types have poorly defined yellowish spots of various sizes. The fins are bright yellow spotted with red.

This variety is prevalent in China, Korea, Japan, and Singapore, but is rare in Europe and the United States.

Celestial
(Also called Heavenward Gazer or Sky-gazer; Japanese: Deme Ranchu)

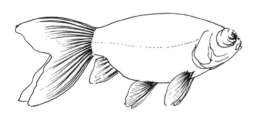

The celestial is truly a marvel among goldfish. Its ancestor is the red telescope eye, and it originated in the Chinese province of Kwangtung.

The body is cylindrical shape, the dorsal fin is absent, and the caudal fin is short and divided. For the most part, these fish are a uniform dark red, but some races have bright yellow ventral and lateral regions.

As the name indicates, the fish's eyes are positioned at an angle of 90° from the body axis, i.e., the fish looks straight up. A thick cuticular connective tissue surrounds the eyeballs. Fingerlings begin to form their unique eyes within a month after hatching. Under favorable conditions, it takes about 10 months for the characteristic eyes to develop completely.

Celestials prefer warmth. Optimum water temperatures during the summer range from 64°–67°F (18°–25°C), and during the winter, 57°–61°F (14°–16°C). Celestial goldfish are among the most expensive and highly prized goldfish in China, Japan, and Singapore. This variety is found less frequently in Europe and the United States. Buddhist monks in Korea often keep celestial goldfish in temple garden ponds.

Bubble Eye

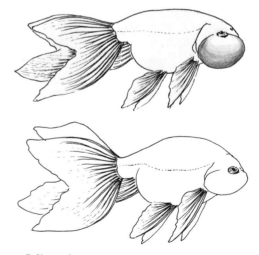

TOP: Calico telescope eye
BOTTOM LEFT: Black moor from a Chinese breeding strain
BOTTOM RIGHT: Dutch lionhead, also known as oranda shishigashira or lionhead veiltail

Bubble eyes are a unique, amazing variety originally from China. The fish is characterized by yellowish sacs on both sides of the head, just below the eyes. These striking bubbles, shaped like grapes, are filled with a mostly opaque fluid. The eyes are located at the base of the bubbles and are directed upward. There is no dorsal fin, and the caudal fin is paired. Most bubble eye goldfish are bright red, but the caudal fin of some individuals is edged with bright yellow.

The variety is extremely delicate and quite rare. Occurring primarily in China, Japan, and Singapore, bubble eyes are found only occasionally in Europe and America, and even then only in small numbers.

Peacock Tail
(Japanese: Jikin)

This very attractive variety from Japan is easy to recognize. Its divided caudal fin, with nearly equally sized upper and lower lobes, is almost vertical to the dorsal midline. The peduncle between both parts of the caudal fin is particularly densely scaled. All fins, the operculum (gill cover), and the tip of the mouth are bright red, especially at spawning time, while the head and body are white tinged with pink.

The fish can be recognized by its movement, which is quite unlike any other fish—it looks as if a peacock were prancing. Peacock tails grow

TOP LEFT: A pearlscale (above) bred in China and a bubble eye (below)
TOP RIGHT: Peacock tail
BOTTOM: A Chinese pompom

very rapidly. Maintained under optimum conditions, they mature within a year.

This is one of the most beautiful and prized goldfish varieties, but it requires constant special care. It likes warm temperatures and does best at water temperatures of 64°–77°F (18°–25°C) in the summer and 59°–68°F (15°–20°C) in the winter. The fish looks magnificent in a light blue bowl or in goldfish ponds. Known primarily in Japan, this variety can be found in small numbers in Europe and the United States.

The Goldfish of Tosa
(Japanese: Tosakin)

This strikingly beautiful variety was developed in Japan from the veiltail goldfish more than a century ago.

Its predominant characteristic is that its fully developed caudal fin does not remain in a vertical position. Instead, the sides of the paired fin curl outward with wavelike motions as the fish swims. Its head narrows toward the tip of the mouth. Body and fins are orange-red, except for a bright yellow border on the caudal fin.

This variety occurs primarily in Japan.

Arrow Tail
(Japanese: Watonai)

This variety was originally bred in Japan more than a century ago from the common domestic goldfish and the veiltail.

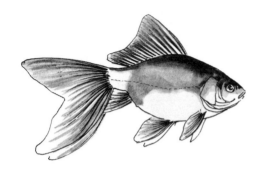

The body of the fish is elongated. The large caudal fin lacks veil characteristics, and its ends narrow into an arrowhead shape. The eyes are normal. The body is bright yellow with a few dark patches, mainly in the ventral region.

The arrow tail is a pleasant sight in a white or black bowl. It is a common and very popular variety in Japan.

Pompom
(with curled operculum and flared nostrils; also called Narial Bouquet or Red Dragon Eye; Japanese type with dorsal: Hanafusa)

This variety, with its rather grotesque appearance, comes from China, and is considered a goldfish marvel.

It resembles the veiltail in shape, but differs in having a striking, bubbly growth resembling a fur hat atop its head. In addition, the stiff operculum does not cover the bright red gill arches completely, so that their rhythmic pulsation is clearly visible. Normally, the fish is bright red with yellow ventral blotches of vari-

ous sizes. The caudal fin has a bright yellow border.

This variety, more arresting than beautiful, is found almost exclusively in China.

Oranda
(Some types also called Redcap or Tigerhead)

Bred in China, this variety is a mutation or derivative of the veiltail.

Its body is thickset. Its major feature is the profusion of puffy, bright red tissue excrescences covering the entire head except for the area beneath the lower jaw. These growths often resemble the caps of certain mushrooms. The pupils are just about all that is visible of the tiny eyes of this fish. Everything else is covered by the silky hood. All of the fins are well-developed and somewhat veillike, and the caudal fin is paired. The body and fins are usually bright red with the exception of the caudal fin, which may be partially or totally colored bright yellow. There are also some lemon-yellow oranda varieties in Japan and lavender ones in China.

The oranda is a splendid sight in white, yellow, or light blue bowls or ponds. This attractive, common variety is found around the world.

Calico Oranda
(Japanese: Azumanishiki)

Calico oranda were first bred in Japan about 40 years ago, when a calico was crossed with an oranda.

The body of the fish is slightly elongated and more compressed than egg-shaped. There are several mushroomlike growths on the head that are usually orange-yellow but are sometimes bright red. Body and fins are bright yellow decorated with spots like those of the calico.

This variety likes warm water—64°–77°F (18°–25°C) in the summer, 57°–68°F (14°–20°C) in the winter. It is most common in Japan but is also known in Europe and North America.

Shubunkin

This variety was first bred in Japan around the turn of the century by crossbreeding a calico and a common domestic goldfish. Crossing a calico and a wildtype goldfish will result in a similar variation.

The variety has an elongated, flattened body. Its single caudal fin makes the shubunkin an unusually agile goldfish. Its eyes are normal, and all its scales are arranged in mosaic fashion. Several color morphs are known, all with one common trait—they have multicolored spots. We know of very light fish, barely "sprinkled," and of others showing extensive red, white, or light blue blotches which are in turn spotted brown or black.

This common variety is found throughout the world.

REQUIREMENTS OF GOLDFISH

In order to make goldfish comfortable in the settings we provide for them, we must be aware of their environmental needs and requirements. In short, we have to provide adequate conditions, particularly as regards heat, light, space, and water quality.

HEAT REQUIREMENTS

Goldfish, according to aquarist terminology, belong to those species that may be kept in "cold water" tanks, as opposed to tropical fish, which require a heated aquarium. This means that the temperature in a goldfish tank may fluctuate within a broad range and that heating is not necessary during the winter. Unfortunately, this general principle holds true nowadays only for the simpler varieties, since most of the prized, exotic goldfish, such as the lionhead, the peacock tail, and so forth, cannot tolerate temperatures below 41°F (5°C) for extended periods of time. While the cold does not actually kill the fish, it lowers their resistance to diseases, makes them susceptible to various circulatory disorders, and results in indigestion, loss of appetite, and fat accumulation. Therefore, it is best to maintain water temperatures for delicate goldfish varieties at 59° to 68°F (15°–20°C) during the winter.

During the summer—the period for reproduction and raising fingerlings—the ideal temperture range for goldfish is 75° to 77°F (24°–25°C). The optimum temperature range for overwintering is 37° to 41°F (4°–5°C). For some varieties, however, the temperature must not be allowed to fall below 57°F (14°C) for any considerable length of time, which means that they are not capable of spending the winter outdoors.

LIGHT REQUIREMENTS

It is just as important for a goldfish hobbyist to know the light rquirements of his or her pets. In nature, goldfish thrive best with morning or late afternoon sun and in so-called "diffused" light, avoiding the intense midday summer sun by hiding under the leaves of aquatic plants or in shadows cast over the water. Direct exposure to bright light over long periods of time disturbs the fish and will have adverse effects sooner or later. For example, too much light can cause some varieties to lose their characteristic features.

SPACE REQUIREMENTS

How many gallons of water do goldfish need? How large a tank is needed for spawning or for raising a hundred fingerlings? These are the sorts of questions constantly arising among goldfish hobbyists, and we will answer at least a few of them in some detail. Basically, the necessary amount of water depends largely on the size and the variety of the goldfish, the method of goldfish keeping, and the temperature. The water in which the fish lives serves:

1. as a medium for gas exchange for respiration (oxygen uptake and carbon dioxide release)
2. as the recipient of waste products and to break down and dissolve those substances resulting from biological processes of the goldfish
3. as the medium in which the fish moves and reacts.

In general, their relatively small requirements for movement and for oxygen allow goldfish to flourish even in cramped living quarters. However, an effort should be made to improve the quality of the water by aerating the tank or by adding aquatic plants, which will, if healthy, assimilate carbon dioxide and produce oxygen.

Insufficient space may result in:
1. respiratory insufficiency—breathing becomes inhibited, the fish are suffocating and try to gasp for more air at the water surface;
2. increased accumulation of slime and waste deposits—as a result, the water becomes murky quickly or, in extreme cases, even foul, and the goldfish are in imminent danger of being poisoned;
3. lethargy, with problems in the organs governing movement and digestion.

Crowding also stunts the growth of young fish even when the fish have adequate food.

The space necessary for the optimum care of goldfish depends upon the methods and objectives of the hobbyist.

For simple maintenance the modest demands of goldfish can be met completely in a small space. If your living room has only a small end table or a similarly confined space available, you may still keep young fish, 1 or 2 inches (2–4 centimeters) long, in a goldfish bowl, either individually or in small groups. Two to 3 quarts of water per fish are adequate. The bowl should never be filled to the brim—there should be at least ½ to ¾ inch (1.5–2 centimeters) between the water surface and the top edge of the container. If you have more room, and if fish complement your room decor, you might consider a bowl holding 1 to 2 gallons, or even more, and populate it with several small fish or a few larger fish. If you prefer to keep fewer, larger fish, then you should consider fish less than 2 to 2¾ inches (5–7 centimeters) long for bowls holding up to 2½ gallons, since fish of that size require 1–2 gallons of water each. More fish, of course, can be kept in larger bowls (2½ to 5 gallons) or in tanks (12 to 125 gallons). Under those conditions, even fully grown individuals,

4 to 6 inches (10–15 centimeters) long, do very well. If you want to keep goldfish in such large containers, however, you will have to consider the difficulty of changing the water in a container of that size. A full-grown goldfish requires approximately 2½ to 7 gallons of water.

Container volume, the total number of goldfish, and the size of the fish are all factors that have a bearing on the frequency with which the water must be changed. The more space available for each individual fish, the less frequently must the water be changed and the container cleaned.

When keeping goldfish just for decoration, one is not trying to raise healthy, strong individuals suitable for breeding. Therefore, space requirements can be greatly reduced. Keeping goldfish in aquariums or tanks follows the principles of natural maintenance; as a result, you have to allow for more space per fish. This is especially true for fish kept outdoors and, above all, for breeding stock. Table 1 presents the amount of water required per goldfish according to the method of maintaining them.

An additional consideration is that many specialized varieties, including lionheads, peacock tails, bubble eyes, and celestials, need more space, a higher quality diet, and warmer water, and are thus not at all suited for small containers.

On the basis of both our own experiences and accounts from Japan, we would like to add some information concerning the spatial needs of newly-hatched goldfish (larvae, fingerlings) and yearlings during the process of maturing in breeding tanks.

As Table 2 shows, a tank with a water depth of 12 inches (30 centimeters) can hold approximately 1000 to 1200 freshly hatched goldfish ¼ inch (6 millimeters) long per 10 square foot (one sq. meter) for 7 to 10 days. At that time, the density of fish will have to be reduced to only 100 to 120 fish ¾ inch (2 centimeters) long. Fifty to sixty fish 2 inches (5 centimeters) long can coexist in that same amount of water, but only 10 to 15 4 inch (10 centimeter) fish.

Goldfish

Table 1. Average water volume required per goldfish in liters (= quarts) at a temperature of 64°F to 77°F (18°–25°C)

Length of fish									
centimeters	2	3	4	5	6	7	8	9	10
inches	0.75	1.25	1.5	2	2.25	2.75	3.25	3.5	4
Type of System									
Bowl	1.5	2	3	5	7	8	10	25	35
Non-aerated aquarium	3	4	5	6	8	10	12	16	30
Aerated aquarium	2	3	3.5	4	5	6	7	8	12
Outdoor goldfish breeding	3–4	4–5	7–8	10–11	16–17	30	40	50	70

Note: The water volume required for more delicate varieties (celestials, peacock tails, lionheads, and bubble eyes) with a length of more than 1¾ to 2 inches (4-5 centimeters) is twice the average. For example, a 2¼ inch (6 centimeter) peacock tail kept in a simple bowl needs 14 liters of water; in an aquarium, it needs 10 to 16 liters, depending on the presence of aeration; for backyard breeding, 32 to 34 liters are required.

Table 2. Total number of goldfish that may be kept per 10 square feet (1 square meter) of surface area in outdoor breeding tanks 12 inches (30 centimeters) deep.

Fish length			Number of fish if the variety is	
inches (approx)	/	centimeters	hardy	delicate
0.25	/	0.6	1500	1000
0.5	/	1.0	1000	500
0.75	/	2.0	200	100
1.25	/	3.0	150	50
1.5	/	4.0	100	50
2.0	/	5.0	60	15
2.25	/	6.0	40	8
2.75	/	7.0	30	5
3.25	/	8.0	25	3
3.5	/	9.0	20	2
4.0	/	10.0	15	1

Note: Delicate varieties include lionheads, peacock tails, celestials, bubble eyes, and redheads.

For individuals of the more demanding varieties longer than about 1½ inch (4 centimeters) sub- tract about 10 to 20% from these values. At such low densities these varieties grow very well and can develop their characteristics to their fullest potential.

WATER QUALITY

As far as water quality is concerned, goldfish are not particularly demanding. In general, plain, clean water is just fine. Rain water, fresh spring water, or well water are generally better suited than chlorinated or fluoridized tap water. Tap water, which is usually all that is available, must be conditioned for goldfish by allowing it to stand awhile, then stirring it vigorously so that it is well aerated. This procedure will remove most of the chlorine. Then, let the water stag- nate for another 24 to 28 hours to become "cured" before using it to replace or replenish the con- tainer's water.

The pH should be close to neutral. Water of pH less than 5 or greater than 9 is not accept- able for keeping goldfish. Water should also be of no more than medium hardness and moderate

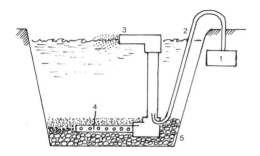

Goldfish tank with bottom filter: 1) air pump, 2) ventilation tube, 3) inflow pipe for clean water, 4) perforated suction pipe, 5) bottom gravel layer

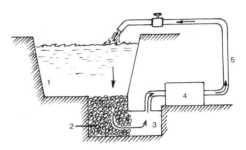

Recirculation and water purification method with bottom filter: 1) tank, 2) bottom filter, 3) water collector, 4) pump, 5) pipe and faucet for clean water

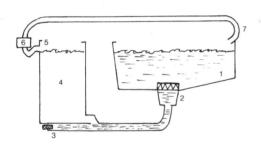

Recirculation tank for outdoor use with suction and filter attachments: 1) tank, 2) suction drain, 3) sludge removal, 4) filter, 5) outflow for clean water, 6) pump, 7) water intake

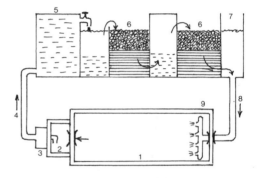

Biological water purification system: 1) goldfish tank, 2) sedimentation tank, 3) water collector, 4) pipe for used water, 5) algae tank, 6) filter (gravel, sand, activated charcoal), 7) purified water container, 8) pipe, 9) inflow jets for clean water

mineral content.

The amount of dissolved oxygen in the water is very important and should be at least 50% of saturation value. Table 3 lists the temperature-dependent saturation values for oxygen. Note that the warmer the water, the less oxygen it contains. Dissolved oxygen can be measured by instruments or chemical techniques, but this is not really necessary in the case of goldfish. They demonstrate a lack of oxygen by their "air-gasping" behavior, and their resistance to oxygen depletion is extremely high. Lack of oxygen can be alleviated by replacing some of the water or by aerating. In cases of chronic oxygen insufficiency, a complete change of water in the bowl or tank is indicated.

Table 3. Oxygen solubility in water at various temperatures	
°F / °C	O_2/mg/1
39 / 4	13
41 / 5	12
50 / 10	11
59 / 15	10
68 / 20	9
77 / 25	8
86 / 30	7
95 / 35	5

A complete exchange of water at regular intervals (not just occasionally when the water quality deteriorates or when oxygen is depleted) is usually done only in cases of simple goldfish keeping, as in a small bowl. Complete exchange is impractical when breeding goldfish in a garden pond. Instead, partial water replacement on a more frequent basis is employed.

Aquarium maintenance, on the other hand, requires only infrequent water changes. In a carefully balanced aquarium, even water several years old can provide the fish with a clean, satisfactory environment. Only the amount of evaporated water needs to be replenished.

Simple goldfish bowls cannot provide or maintain the biological balance necessary for satisfactory water quality because of a lack of plants. This means that the water in such containers must be changed every 7 to 10 days. This is particularly true for goldfish bowls inside the home; water in outdoor containers needs to be replaced less frequently due to the effects of wind, sunlight, and the algae found in these containers. Before changing the water you should transfer your goldfish temporarily to a smaller container such as a Mason jar or bucket filled with "cured" water. Then you can empty the original container, wash it out thoroughly, and refill it with fresh water. If you have plants, wash them, too, before returning them along with the fish. Take care to minimize the temperature difference between old and new water—it should not exceed 5° to 7°F (3°–4°C). After the water change, the goldfish will turn pale, but only temporarily.

Water replacement is also essential in backyard breeding tanks, even if the goldfish appear to be getting along well in the old water. Such a water change removes a significant portion of the fishes' waste products and controls the growth of algae.

Water in breeding tanks is usually changed in a way that lets the goldfish remain in their containers. You may either pump out 30% or 40% of the old water and replace it with fresh water, or let fresh water flow through the tank until 30% to 40% of the old water has been exchanged. Take care not to add too much water at one time to prevent an extreme or rapid temperature drop in excess of 5°F to 7°F (3°C–4°C). The practical way is to add only small quantities of water to your fish tank, if possible at midday, over an extended period of time. These partial exchanges are generally needed every two weeks or more frequently if the water gets too warm or turns green, or if the fish indicate lack of oxygen early in the morning.

It is essential for steady growth and development that goldfish get fresh water on time. Old, unreplenished water can often lead to serious diseases.

METHODS FOR KEEPING GOLDFISH

There are three basic methods for keeping goldfish. Your decision as to which method you will use must be based on considerations of space, money and the amount of time you are able to devote to your goldfish. The methods are:
1. simple goldfish maintenance (bowl);
2. aquarium maintenance and goldfish breeding;
3. breeding goldfish in an outdoor garden setting.

Of course, these three methods can be combined to some extent. For example, you might keep your fish in garden tanks during the summer (method 3) and transfer them to an aquarium (method 2), or even to variously-sized bowls (method 1) for the winter.

Let us take a closer look at these three methods.

In a Bowl

This is the oldest method, and is very common in China to this day. Goldfish kept in this way require very little care. Normally, the method is used only for keeping just a few gold-

Pearlscale of Chinese origin

fish intended to decorate an apartment, office space, or garden. Smaller containers such as ceramic or glass bowls are most often used; occasionally, larger earthenware vessels, basins, or small fountains are used. Goldfish in such containers can be viewed only from above, except if they are in glass bowls. Therefore, varieties with a particularly interesting "top view," such as telescope eyes and veiltails, are most suited for this method. This method precludes breeding, serving only ornamental purposes. Use adult individuals for best results and easiest care. The method requires about as much care and time as your simplest potted plant. Care consists mainly of feeding, cleaning the goldfish container, and occasional replenishing of water lost by evaporation. The simple method is thus recommended whenever the fish are serving a decorative purpose and when minimum care is one of the objectives.

In an Aquarium

This method requires a little more time and effort, and is particularly well suited for goldfish watching. A goldfish aquarium is equipped like any other aquarium, except that the understanding goldfish do not require a heater or aerator if the aquarium is not overcrowded. An aquarium offers a side view of the fish; this method is thus recommended for fish that look attractive when viewed from the side, such as classic veiltail forms, peacock tails, pearlscales, lionheads, and orandas.

Breeding usually occurs only in outdoor tanks, but you may get lucky in an aquarium setting. If you'd like to breed, you'll need a large aquarium (37 to 50 gallons or 150 to 200 liters), because the fish do not reproduce in a confined space. Keeping goldfish this way can become more than just an entertaining pastime. A goldfish aquarium can hold fish of different ages and sizes at the same time, letting you get involved,

TOP: White oranda
BOTTOM: Calico oranda

in theory at least, in all stages of breeding, growth, and development. You can have all this with a minimum of expense and equipment, and with a fish species not only easy to keep but also very versatile from the standpoint of breeding. It is often said that keeping and breeding goldfish in an aquarium is the training ground for more scientifically-oriented aquarists.

In an Outdoor Pond

Breeding goldfish in your backyard corresponds roughly to the classical Chinese and Japanese way of keeping goldfish—the ultimate academy of goldfish culture. The largest modern Japanese and Chinese breeding facilities for goldfish match the freshwater fish hatching industry in terms of the quantity of fish produced. Millions of goldfish are raised for beginners who want to keep goldfish according to the first two methods.

This particular method requires precise biological knowledge. Its objective, apart from simple breeding, is to raise goldfish to various ages and to refine the stock by controlled and selective means. Another requirement is a uniform, first-class breeding stock. All of your specimens must be of high breeding quality and have good potential if you are to succeed. Devoted goldfish breeders concentrate on a single variety, expanding breeding to at most two or three other varieties. You should always choose the cream of the crop as the parents in your breeding attempts. What goldfish variety you choose depends on your own personal taste and, unfortunately, on the limitations of the current goldfish supply. At the time of this writing, most small-scale Japanese breeders were concentrating on lionheads.

Goldfish breeding in the backyard takes place in open-air tanks or ponds. Even the simplest breeding procedures require at least two or three tanks: one for breeding, one for raising the fingerlings, and one for keeping the breeding stock. This means that you have to create a small hatchery tank system in your yard. You will need suitable plantings, a way of protecting the fish from nocturnal visitors (cats, rats, raccoons), adequate plumbing, and some provision for overwintering.

This brief overview shows that keeping goldfish in a garden setting entails detailed planning. For that reason, the method is recommended primarily for more commercial or semi-commercial, professionally-oriented breeders, or for those dedicated goldfish lovers who can devote a lot of time to their pets—and who have large yards.

PRACTICAL ASPECTS OF GOLDFISH KEEPING

Let us now consider containers for simple goldfish maintenance, aquariums, and finally breeding tanks for use in the backyard.

CONTAINERS FOR SIMPLE GOLDFISH MAINTENANCE

Containers for simple goldfish care come in all shapes and sizes. The main consideration is always that the container provide a good view of your goldfish. The main reason for this method of keeping goldfish is, after all, to enjoy them as objects of beauty.

As already mentioned, goldfish differ from tropical fish in their versatility with respect to care and "housing." While tropical fish thrive only in aquariums with a water temperature of 68 to 79°F (20°–26°C), goldfish do well in a variety of pots, bowls, jars, tanks, and basins, and in a wide range of temperatures. Let us re-emphasize that confining quarters and lack of

Suitable shapes for ceramic and earthenware goldfish bowls

49

Goldfish

Suitable shapes for glass goldfish containers

vegetation are neither harmful nor cruel to goldfish.

In the home an attractive ceramic bowl is an excellent choice for keeping goldfish, but various glass bowls are just as suitable. Although plastic bowls are admittedly not so stylish, they are unbreakable, and are therefore practical for children's goldfish.

Basically, bowls at least 3 to 4 inches (8–10 centimeters) deep are ideal for keeping goldfish; just watch that the container wall is no more than 10 to 12 inches (25–30 centimeters) high. In addition, undecorated bowls with a smooth inner surface display the shape and movement of the goldfish clearly and effectively.

The size of the bowl depends primarily on the space available. In this respect, the goldfish bowl is like any other object or piece of furniture in your home: its form, color, and size should be in harmony with its setting. In a small room, for example, you will not want a goldfish container the size of a barrel. On the other hand, a small bowl will be visually lost in a large room.

A small goldfish can be kept in as little as 1½ to 2 quarts (liters) of water. A container holding that amount of water thus represents the minimum size for a goldfish bowl. The typical diameter of such a bowl is 7 to 8 inches (18–20 centimeters), its height 4 to 6 inches (10–15 centimeters). Goldfish bowls suitable for the home range from this smallest size to containers up to 4 to 5 gallons (15–20 liters) capacity. In larger spaces such as a conservatory or a stairway landing, even larger containers may look very pleasing, although they should be made of artificial stone or cement.

In addition, there is a trend toward keeping goldfish in decorative tanks or basins within the home, and in some countries artificial stone containers in gardens and parks, originally intended as flower pots, are being used as goldfish bowls.

The examples in the illustration on page 49 can serve only as a guideline, of course, since the variety of container sizes and shapes is practically endless.

The color of the bowl is at least as important as its shape. The external surface should harmonize with the colors surrounding it. The interior color of the bowl should set off the color of your goldfish. For example, a reddish goldfish would be almost invisible against the background of a red bowl; green, black, or white would be more suitable. On the other hand, black goldfish have a stunning effect on a red background.

A smooth interior simplifies your cleaning chores considerably. The rough glaze of many ceramic bowls makes cleaning and removal of deposits very difficult. A small, hard brush or an old toothbrush comes in handy if you have such a bowl.

Bowls for simple goldfish care usually contain nothing but water, but you may add a graceful, floating aquatic plant. A few branches of delicate pond-weed look equally nice. In a bright location, the plants will produce oxygen, which is beneficial to the fish. If the bowl is in a dark or shaded location, you should do without plants since they would add to the build up of carbon dioxide, necessitating more frequent water changes. Don't cover the bottom with soil or sand—you can accentuate the beauty of your fish by a little coarse colored gravel or a few small rocks.

The water should be clean and conditioned—your fish will die in highly chlorinated tap water. Let the water stand for a few days to get rid of the chlorine. As far as acidity, alkalinity, and water hardness is concerned, goldfish really have no special requirements. Any water that can be used as drinking water is quite suitable as goldfish water.

Maintenance of simple goldfish bowls does not present any problems. The most important task is cleaning the bowl when you change the water.

THE GOLDFISH AQUARIUM

Goldfish do not thrive in deep aquariums. Therefore the water depth should not exceed 10 to 12 inches (25–30 centimeters), the optimum being 8 or 9 inches (20–22 centimeters). Depth requirements also determine the surface area, since aquariums look best when their height exceeds their width. Accordingly, popular dimensions (L × W × H) are 20 × 10 × 12 inches (50 × 25 × 30 centimeters) which holds 10 gallons (37 liters), and 16 × 8 × 10 inches (40 × 20 × 25 centimeters), which contains 5½ gallons (20 liters). Keep larger fish in 15-gallon (63-liter) containers, which measure 24 × 12 × 12 inches (70 × 30 × 30 centimeters) or in 20-gallon 74 liters) tanks, which measure 24 × 12 × 16 inches (70 × 30 × 35 centimeters). Large, shallow aquariums (i.e., 40 × 24 × 14 inches, or 100 × 60 × 35 centimeters) are more suitable for breeding and raising young.

Aquariums with capacities of up to 120 to 150 gallons (500–600 liters) are usually made of glass panes assembled with sealing compounds. The larger the aquarium, the thicker the glass. Guidelines for building aquariums can be found in a number of specialized publications, and we do not have to go into that subject at length here.

Another type of goldfish container, the goldfish globe or similar glass container, from the "golden age" of goldfish at the turn of the century, should at least be mentioned. The globe was the predecessor of the modern aquarium, and the first container to offer a side view of the fish. Besides these old-fashioned globes, bowls, or glasses, other kinds of glassware (a punch bowl, for example) can offer your fish a comfortable home. The volume of such spherical goldfish containers is generally 3 to 6 quarts (liters).

A goldfish aquarium or a glass globe is harder to set up than the simple bowls treated in the previous section. They usually must be provided with bottom fill, plants, perhaps artificial lighting, and, depending on the goldfish variety, even an aerator.

Since most goldfish like to feed on the bottom, the aquarium floor should be covered with a 1 to 1½ inch (3–4 centimeter) layer of well-washed sand or gravel. It is usual to have the sand or gravel slope slightly towards one corner of the aquarium or, in case of a round container, towards the middle, both for appearance and to simplify the collection and removal of excretions and deposits.

Rocks with rough surfaces or sharp edges do not belong in any goldfish container since they may injure delicate fins and scrape off scales. Likewise, plants must be chosen with care. Plants with finely dissected leaves and a supple, silky appearance—for example, *Cabomba aquatica, Myriophyllum* species, *Elodea, Fontinalis*—are best for goldfish. Sharp-edged or stiff plants, such as hornwort, are not appropriate for a goldfish aquarium since they, too, can damage fish fins. Besides, delicate-leaved plants look much better with goldfish.

Aquarium maintenance, which is a little more involved, is described in several excellent books on the subject that include helpful tips on goldfish aquariums in particular. Some of these publications are included in the bibliography at the end of this book.

OUTDOOR TANKS

Garden tanks, for our purposes, include outdoor tanks suitable for breeding goldfish, even the more demanding varieties. They do not include the stone containers you might keep in your garden for ornamental purposes, nor the pools or basins of fountains, nor ornamental ponds. Such containers have already been discussed in the section on simple goldfish keeping.

Breeding tanks may be made of artificial stone or plastic, and may be built into the ground or fashioned from prepared molds. A sunken tank is stationary, while a molded above-ground tank has the advantage that it can be moved if necessary.

The first task in setting up breeding containers is to select a suitable location. One important consideration is that the water surface be exposed to the sun for about five hours per day from May through September, preferably including midday sun. The long axis of the tank should run from north to south. Another consideration is the desirability of protecting the tank (and the fish) from cold prevailing (usually north) winds. Trees, shrubs, or even a wall serve this purpose very well.

In addition to considering the tank's requirements, you should avoid letting the goldfish tank(s) disrupt the overall design of your garden. You may want to get a few tips and ideas from readily available literature on the role of water in garden design. A sunken cement tank is probably your best choice. A fiberglass tank, which is considerably more expensive, can likewise be sunk into the ground. Recently, sunken tanks made of corrosion-free metal plates have become available, but they are very costly. Whatever you decide on, remember that the sides of a sunken tank should extend about 3 to 5 inches (8–12 centimeters) above ground level.

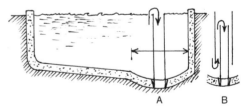

Cross section of an outdoor goldfish pool made of cement: A) overflow pipe for surface water removal, B) sheathed drain

You get exactly what you want if you build your own sunken reinforced concrete tank. Many of the more sophisticated manuals on landscape design explain how to build such a tank.

For controlling the water level and to provide efficient drainage, install a drain and overflow pipe at the lowest point of the tank. This pipe has to serve two functions: you want to be able to drain water from the water's surface as well as from the tank bottom. Secure the drain with wire mesh to avoid having your small fish drain off with the water. The accompanying illustration clearly shows how you can draw off water from the surface as well as from the bottom, and how water can be diverted without an actual overflow pipe. Without a bottom drain, water must be siphoned off. This is very difficult and has the disadvantage that permanently-installed tanks can never be emptied completely, although they must be, from time to time, for cleaning.

You can also fashion excellent, beautiful breeding tanks from rectangular plant containers of artificial stone. Ordinarily these planters are produced without a drain, but you can custom-order them from the manufacturer with top and bottom drains. You can even drill your own openings with a concrete chisel, and then use resin to install a cylindrical connecting drain pipe. Breeding tanks made from planters are not put into the ground.

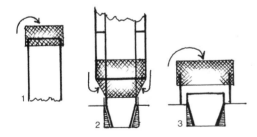

Covers for goldfish tank drains: 1) gauze ring for surface water removal, 2) gauze cover for bottom water removal, 3) gauze drum on drain opening

A general rule for selecting the size of a goldfish breeding tank is that the water depth should be approximately 8 inches (20 centimeters) for young fish and 10 to 12 inches (25–30 centimeters) for adult fish. Typical sizes of breeding tanks range from 36 by 48 inches (90 × 120 centimeters) to 72 × 108 inches (180 × 270 centimeters).

Smaller tanks are usually used for keeping yearlings (fry), larger ones for older fish. It is more efficient to build the tanks right next to each other for better use of space and to simplify water supply, drainage.

Don't cover the bottom of outdoor tanks with soil or sand. You may add a few submerged pond-weeds in shallow, smooth flower pots as hiding places for the fish. Dense vegetation, particularly floating aquatic plants, is more suitable for ornamental fish ponds.

One important consideration is a good water supply. The more intensively you wish to pursue goldfish breeding, the greater the need for filling your tank. Ideally, the tank should be filled from a second tank used to "cure" the water for several days. If tap water is all that is available, wait for two or three days before returning the goldfish to the freshly filled tank.

Finally, give your breeding tank a pretty setting by planting suitable garden plants around it. Depending on your climate, reeds and flowering rush, or possibly a willow, will make a perfect frame for an even more beautiful goldfish tank arrangement.

CARE OF OUTDOOR BREEDING TANKS

Care of outdoor goldfish tanks differs markedly from the care required for indoor containers and aquariums.

Changing the water from time to time and replacing water lost to evaporation and seepage is one of the most important aspects of tank maintenance. Any seepage can be detrimental and disruptive to your breeding efforts, since a constantly falling water level makes the fish restless. Replenishing the water of a leaking tank is only a temporary solution; the cause of the seepage must be eliminated as soon as possible. A quick and safe method is to coat the source of the leak several times with liquid asphalt.

Remove sludge and detritus on the tank bottom whenever you change the water. This is easily done with a rubber or plastic siphon hose.

Suction device for sludge removal

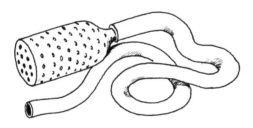

Suction tube with perforated plastic bottle to prevent the fish from escaping

Be careful not to siphon away your fish, especially the fry. To avoid losing fish you can protect the suction opening with a perforated plastic plug or a box with wire mesh sides. Sludge removal is faster and easier if the bottom of the tank slopes down to a place where debris will collect. Naturally, siphoning is only possible if the discharge end of the hose is below the bottom of the tank.

Cleaning sunken tanks in this manner is just about impossible. You need a suction device in order to remove the deposits on the bottom of a sunken tank. This method, of course, takes more time than siphoning.

During the period of maximum solar radiation (from about the middle of May to the middle of August in most areas), you should provide shade for the tanks at least during the hottest hours. You can make a permanent screen from a rush mat woven loosely enough to permit diffuse sunlight to fall on the water surface. Another solution is to cover about a third of the tank with densely woven reed matting. The extent of the shade you need will be apparent from the condition of the water. A green tinge to the water, murkiness, and oxygen deficiency in the mornings, if they persist, indicate that the tank gets too much light. In this event, additional shade and more frequent water changes are necessary.

It is also important to protect your goldfish from predators. Slow-moving or stationary goldfish are easy prey for cats, rats, raccoons, and even birds. Even normally vegetarian wild ducks can harm the fish with their beaks. You can protect the fish by covering the tank with a wire screen on a wood or metal frame; normal chicken wire offers adequate protection. The wire frame is usually removed by day—largely for aesthetic reasons.

Disinfection which serves to prevent disease and to ward off parasites, is another important aspect of tank care. Disinfect your tank whenever you empty it. Obviously, disinfection is also necessary whenever you notice any symptoms of disease or infestation.

To disinfect the tank, first rinse it with clear water. Scrub the entire inside with a good, hard brush, paying special attention to corners and

A splendid adult oranda (red-yellow form)

edges. Following another rinse with plenty of water, apply a concentrated solution of table salt to the walls with a soft brush and let the tank dry. If you are pressed for time, wash the sides again with a 0.1% solution of malachite green. This increases the effectiveness of the disinfection process considerably. When the breeding cycle is completed, the tank should be disinfected in the same manner. The most effective method, if time and season permit, is to let the cleansed and disinfected tank dry out completely, and to expose the dry tank to sub-freezing winter temperatures. If there are any remnants of sediment on the bottom, the tank will not dry completely. In that case freezing will not be as effective, since the germs are capable of surviving in the frozen, water-saturated sludge. If you cannot get your tank totally dry, you'll have to disinfect it again in the spring with salt and malachite.

Removing leaves and other floating debris is a matter of course; it is one of the daily tasks of caring for your goldfish tanks.

OVERWINTERING

Overwintering is really only a potential problem for goldfish kept outdoors. For goldfish in indoor bowls and aquariums, which remain in the same place all year round, overwintering is not an issue.

There are several ways to help goldfish living in garden tanks through the winter, and you want to choose the safest one for your particular situation and variety. One option is to leave the fish outside. Another, is to transfer them to unheated (but not freezing) indoor locations (cellars or other unheated rooms). A third option is to let them spend the winter in heated rooms. The most refined and delicate varieties

TOP AND BOTTOM LEFT: Calico oranda
BOTTOM RIGHT: Shubunkin

(lionheads, peacock tails, etc.) cannot withstand the long, hard winters found across much of the United States. While goldfish do not die immediately of the cold, as tropical fish do, low temperatures weaken them and thus encourages disease. For that reason, individuals of these sensitive varieties should be kept at temperatures of 57°–63°F (14°–18°C) from the beginning of November to the end of March or the middle of April.

One of the prerequisites for successful overwintering is proper preparation of the fish at the end of summer and during the fall. This consists primarily of extra good care and plenty of high-quality food. The goldfish's appetite decreases rapidly below a temperature of 59°F (15°C); at 43°–46°F (6°–8°C), feeding virtually stops. That means that fish kept outdoors will hardly feed at all from mid-November to mid-March. Although their metabolic functions are also greatly reduced, however, they are still slowly consuming energy. This energy is supplied by food reserves (fat and carbohydrates) accumulated in the body prior to the overwintering period. An optimum diet in the preceding months is therefore extremely important for storing the needed reserves.

Goldfish overwintering in an environment warmer than about 46°F (8°C), on the other hand, feed throughout the cold season. For them, good health is crucial in order to ward off parasites (e.g. white spot disease), a common occurrence when fish enter a new environment. A basic rule-of-thumb for any of the three overwintering methods is that only healthy, robust goldfish can survive the winter unharmed.

Goldfish must also be prepared medically. Before the onset of winter, inspect your fish thoroughly. If there is any hint of a parasite infestation, treat the fish immediately. In addition, wash and disinfect the tank in which the fish will spend the winter very carefully before transferring your fish.

Let us consider the three overwintering methods for goldfish in a little more detail.

57

Goldfish

Outdoors

In this method the goldfish spend the cold part of the year in the same tank used for keeping and breeding them during the summer. Table 4 presents the space requirements of overwintering fish. The tank should be protected against severe frost. As long as the temperature remains above freezing, you may leave the tank uncovered. Otherwise, cover the tank with layers of reeds, rush, styrofoam, boards, tarpaper, or other insulating materials. An additional cover of plastic or tarpaper keeps the reeds from collecting too much moisture. Leave a small opening, covered by glass, in this cover so that light can penetrate and so that you can check your goldfish from time to time. For every 10 square feet (1 square meter) of surface area there should be a window of about 6 to 12 square inches (40–80 square centimeters). While the windows will have to be kept clear of snow, a snow blanket on the rest of the cover is beneficial because it effectively improves heat insulation. A carefully covered tank seldom freezes; at most, it will form a very thin layer of ice.

Outside tanks rarely need to be replenished with water during the winter (goldfish should never overwinter in leaking tanks). Fill the tank with clean, fresh water in late fall. If you top it off with enough water before the frost sets in and before the tank is covered, the water will usually last until spring.

Goldfish should not be taken out of the water in sub-freezing temperatures because freezing causes irreparable damage to their skin and fins. Fish kept in outdoor tanks do not need to be fed during the winter months.

In sunny, mild weather you can remove the tank cover part way around noon. Sunlight strengthens the resistance of fish to disease and helps to maintain a healthy oxygen/carbon dioxide balance in the water.

Toward the end of March, as winter approaches its end and weather permits, take the cover off. Do it little by little, at first removing it only during the daytime, later leaving it off overnight. Finally, when the water temperature exceeds 46°–50°F (8°–10°C), leave the tank completely uncovered at all times. Most importantly, check your goldfish at this time for any health problems. Separate sick, abnormally swimming fish from healthy individuals. If you detect a problem, treat the entire population.

Start feeding your goldfish again when the water temperature exceeds 46°F (8°C). They should receive as much food as they can easily consume within half a day. We highly recommend live food, such as tubifex worms, during these first weeks of spring.

Table 4. Total number of goldfish able to overwinter per 10 square inches (1 square meter) surface area of an outdoor tank (16 inches, or 40 centimeters, water depth) without aeration and supplemental water. (The fish population may be increased by 15% if aeration is provided.)

Fish length in inches / cm (approx.)		Total number of fish per 10 sq ft (1 m²)
1½	4	250
2¼	6	200
3¼	8	150
4	10	100

Introducing air bubbles into the tank by means of a thin tube and an electrical aquarium aerator is an additional safety measure because it prevents the formation of ice.

In Unheated Rooms

In this method the goldfish overwinter in plastic, cement, or even metal tanks in rooms with little or no heat, and with an average temperature of approximately 50°F (10°C); the temperature should never drop as low as 32°F (0°C). At 50°F goldfish become inactive, are barely moving and barely eating. Still, they have to be fed. The best food during the winter is tubifex worms, which can be purchased in most pet shops.

Transfer the fish indoors before the onset of severe frost. The tank should not be more than 24 to 28 inches (60–70 centimeters) deep. Table 5 presents the space requirements of this method. If at all possible, aerate the water. Watch for parasites. An above-average overwintering temperature encourages the spread of parasites at a time when the vitality and disease-resistance of the goldfish are already reduced.

A partial water exchange may be necessary now and then. You can usually tell when it is time for a change by the behavior of the fish. They become restless, leave the tank bottom, and frequently swim along the tank walls. Such behavior warns of oxygen-deficient water even before the fish begin gasping for air at the surface. Exhibited regularly, this behavior indicates that considerable quantities of waste products have already accumulated in the water. The goldfish tank should never be allowed to deteriorate to such an extent. Relatively rapid loss of water quality is almost inevitable with this overwintering method. It happens because the balance necessary for good water quality cannot be maintained in such an artificial environment. At the relatively low temperatures and poor light conditions involved you can't even add aquatic plants to the tank to help matters. But you can improve water quality considerably with an efficient filter/aerator system. We recommend these technical aids primarily to avoid too frequent water changes.

This overwintering method is also suitable for the more delicate varieties of goldfish.

In Heated Tanks

This method requires some expert knowledge, a little more effort, and some expense. But it is also the best method. The fish winter in heated rooms (e.g., a greenhouse) or in containers provided with special heaters. Rooms with abundant sun exposure are best. A large aquarium is excellent for this method because light can enter from all sides, allowing algae to grow freely. The water temperature in heated containers should be maintained above 68°F (20°C) all winter long, with the optimum temperature range being 73°–77°F (23°–25°C). Goldfish are active at these temperatures; they must be fed according to their appetite and they must have adequate room in order to develop and grow properly. As a result, substantially fewer fish can be kept in a given amount of water than with the two other methods, as Table 5 shows.

Winter food should be of the same high quality as the normal summer diet. In addition to tubifex worms, which are always available, we

Table 5. Goldfish overwintering in frost-protected (46°–50°F = 8°–10°C) and heated (68°–72°F = 20°–22°C) environments with and without aeration.

Fish length		Water requirement per fish in quarts (liters) at a temperature of			
in inches / cm (approx.)		50°F (10°C)		72°F (22°C)	
		without aeration / with aeration		without aeration / with aeration	
1½	4	4	3	5	5
2¼	6	8	4	10	8
3¼	8	10	6	30	20
4	10	20	15	40	30

recommend frozen plankton.

Since it is beneficial for all goldfish to spend a couple of weeks of every year in colder water, don't initiate the heated wintering process until late fall or early winter. Move the more delicate varieties to the heated containers early in November, and leave the other fish outdoors until early December. Remember, however, that sudden temperature changes are harmful to goldfish. You must adjust the goldfish to their warmer environment slowly over a period of several days. Remove them from their outdoor tanks with some of the original water so that the water can warm up slowly. Over several days, raise the temperature little by little until it passes 68°F (20°C).

Checking the health of your goldfish and treating them for diseases is just as essential with warm overwintering as with the other methods.

Because of the rapidly growing algae, water purity is generally no problem. Nevertheless, aeration and occasional filtration will have noticeably positive effects. If the water becomes too murky because of algal growth, replace part of it. It is important not to lower the overall temperature in the process, because a sudden temperature drop can easily cause digestion problems in goldfish which may, in turn, develop into a host of other diseases. And it is much harder to control disease in these artificial environments than during the summer.

Goldfish that spend the winter in heated tanks must be gradually readjusted to cooler water temperatures in the spring. Therefore, start turning down the heat in early April. When the water temperature in outdoor tanks reaches 50°–54°F (10°–12°C), you can transfer the more delicate varieties back to those tanks. This process of acclimation in the spring helps prepare the goldfish for breeding. In fact, it is vital for the breeding stock since it facilitates an even development of gonads in all fish. To synchronize the rate at which the goldfish will mature to a summer breeding state with the spring warming

trend, the overwintering water should be cooled down gradually, as described above.

As part of a study conducted during the winter of 1972/73, we compared these three overwintering methods. The results clearly showed that wintering in a warm, sunny environment was best. Goldfish that spent the greater part of the winter in aquariums at 68°F (20°C) were double or triple the size of their siblings wintering in cold tanks. Following a cooling-down period in the fall, goldfish in a warm environment soon become "a whole new fish," in the sense that scale color intensifies and the distinctive markings of each particular variety—especially hoods, characteristic fins, and bubble eyes—develop considerably better. Young fish maintained throughout the winter in warm water on a good diet can reproduce successfully at the completion of their first year instead of the two years normally required.

Our research also tested the effects of combining the three methods. The most effective method, but also the one requiring the most care and effort, is to keep the goldfish in heated surroundings throughout the winter. More cold-resistant varieties can be kept in an unheated, but frost-protected, location for one, two, or even three months. After that, they, too, are transferred to a heated environment. Spring is pushed ahead somewhat for them, so to speak. The result is that the fish are in much better condition when the real spring arrives. You might say that, as a rule, all goldfish do better if they spend the winter in a heated tank. For the more sensitive varieties, in fact, a heated environment is a necessity for at least threefourths of the winter. The benefits of active overwintering can be fully achieved only if the goldfish are exposed to the natural light cycle. Ideally, therefore, goldfish should spend the winter in heated conservatories, greenhouses, or glassed-in porches. Our experiments showed that artificial light having the same composition as sunlight did not yield as good results as did natural sunlight in a greenhouse. Such costly wintering procedures are worthwhile primarily if you are keeping the more delicate varieties. The simpler methods suffice for the less demanding varieties which many goldfish hobbyists now keep for breeding purposes. Always remember that proper overwintering is the key to successful goldfish breeding.

SHIPPING GOLDFISH

Goldfish are among the most widely-traveled animals. They have been taken to every corner of the world, have been traded, imported, and exported. Just consider how long it must have taken the first goldfish to reach Europe from China by ship in 1691. Today, such distances are no longer a problem for goldfish shipping.

Air freight is the most common means of transportation across and between countries. Goldfish usually travel in 4 or 5 gallon (15 to 19 liter) transparent polyethylene bags half-filled with water, and inflated with oxygen at a slightly higher-than-normal pressure. The taut bags are enclosed in corrugated cardboard, and within this double protection goldfish can easily travel around the world. Japanese fish breeders developed the process, which is now almost universally applied not just for goldfish—with which it has withstood the test of time—but also for transporting commercial food fishes. For example, our 1963 shipment of several million fish fry from Japan arrived safely in Hungary by

this means. The method works just as well for shipments by rail or road.

When oxygen is pumped into the plastic bags above the water surface, 5 or 6 fish 1½ inches (4 centimeters) long, or 2 or 3 fish 3 or 4 inches (8–10 centimeters) long, or a single 5 inch (12 centimeter) fish can be transported per quart (liter) of water. Goldfish in such bags can be shipped at a temperature of 64°–68°F (18°–20°C) for three to five hours.

If you are unable to supply oxygen to the bags, then give the fish twice as much water, or use colder water. You can ship 30% to 35% more fish per quart at 50°F (10°C). At 41°F (5°C), you can ship 70% more fish per quart than at 64°–68°F (18°–20°C).

A basic rule for shipping fish is never to ship any sick or freshly fed fish. Before you pack your goldfish, let them go without food for one or two days. This is especially crucial should the transit exceed a very few hours because the waste products from insufficiently starved fish will begin to dissolve in the water of the plastic bag. This will cause a shortage, or even depletion, of oxygen in no time. In extreme cases, the toxicity can result in severe, even lethal, poisoning.

Before and during transit, as well as during unloading, make sure that the goldfish are not subjected to any shock or rough handling. Individuals getting ready to spawn are especially sensitive. Correct shipping is crucial for any serious goldfish breeder.

DIET AND FEEDING

INGESTION AND DIGESTION

Goldfish are non-aggressive omnivores. Their mouths are pointed (terminal) and can be extended forward, like that of the carp, in accordion-fashion. This helps the fish search for food in the muddy bottoms of ponds or lakes. In goldfish varieties with altered head shapes the mouth structure may be altered as well. Lionheads, for example, have a small mouth poorly adapted to bottom feeding.

Goldfish have well-developed senses of smell and taste which enable them to search out food easily. The gill arches at the back of the mouth are provided with characteristic chambered pockets that filter and retain food so that it cannot be washed back into the water.

The region well back in the throat, in front of the gullet, has peculiarly arranged pharyngeal teeth that serve to grind up harder elements of a goldfish's diet, such as plant fibers and seeds.

The gullet is short. Goldfish do not have actual stomachs; rather, the gullet leads into the midgut, or mid-intestine, which connects to the rectum. The inner walls of the intestinal tract are covered by mucous membranes rich in enzyme-producing glands. The gall bladder opens into the midgut. There is no distinct pancreas, merely localized cell aggregations in the vicinity of the small intestine. The rectum is short and leads directly to the anal opening.

TYPES OF FOOD

Recently hatched larvae absorb their nourishment from their yolk sacs. After using most of the yolk they become fry, and start to seek all of their food in the water. Initially, they feed primarily on tiny rotifers (Rotatoria) and copepod (*Cyclops*) larvae (0.05–0.2 millimeters), and a small amount of unicellular algae. When the goldfish reach a size of about ⅓ inch (8–9 millimeters), they change their diet to water fleas (*Daphnia*) (0.2–0.4 millimeters), juvenile copepods (0.1–0.6 millimeters) and copepod larvae, and, when kept in culture, to artificially raised brine shrimp larvae.

Goldfish longer than ⅜ inch (1 centimeter) feed on larger juvenile copepods (0.4–1.0 millimeter). As a supplement to animal foods the young fish also require plants, especially algae. They enjoy nibbling on sphagnum moss, which, given sufficient sunlight, grows well on the walls of breeding tanks.

Fish ⅝ to 1¼ inch (1.5–3 centimeters) long are able to feed on adult copepods, medium-sized *Daphnia*, and tubifex worms mashed through a strainer.

Goldfish larger than 1¼ inch (3 centimeters) are ready for all kinds of copepods, *Daphnia* (some of which can be dried), whole tubifex worms, insect larvae (*Chironomus*), ground meat, and microworms (*Enchytraeus albidus*), the latter in small quantities, or the goldfish will get too fat. Adult goldfish should get the same diet. Since they are no longer growing, however, adults need less animal foods. Complement their diet with foods rich in carbohydrates, such as ground barley, wheat, corn, and rice. These grains should comprise a maximum of 30% of the fish's total food intake.

If you are not able to supply your fry with enough live rotifers or copepods, you have to substitute prepared foods. Mash a hard-boiled egg in a glass or china cup and mix it with a little water. Go easy with this yellow, creamlike substance, though. Too much of it can pollute and spoil the tank water within a few hours. The diet of goldfish over 1¼ inch (3 centimeters) long can be supplemented by commercial preparations (e.g. Tetramin, Tetrafin, Wardley's, Blue Ribbon, San Francisco Bay Brand, and others).

FOOD SUPPLY

A large number of goldfish foods, for example, live or dried *Daphnia,* tubifex worms, and commercial preparations are readily available in pet shops and grocery stores. Do not feed your goldfish with any grains treated or disinfected with chemicals.

Food Gathering in the Wild

You can usually catch copepods, *Daphnia,* and insect larvae in clean natural bodies of water such as lakes and swamps—even ditches will do sometimes. We do not recommend getting these live foods from fish ponds, although they are abundant there. You might inadvertently contaminate your fish with dangerous parasites, such as *Bothriocephalus* and *Lernaea.* For collecting, use a tapered plankton net approximately 8 to 10 inches (20–25 centimeters) in diameter and about 12 to 16 inches (30–40 centimeters) long. The net should be made of silk or artificial gauze. Gauze is classified by mill numbers, which describe the "porosity," or size of the mesh apertures. Any mill number between 6 and 20 will retain living organisms while letting water pass freely. The gauze, although not cheap, can often be obtained in hardware or farm supply stores. Assembled nets are available from biological supply houses.

Food gathered in the wild should be brought home in the original water. At home, you can sort the food, feed it to your goldfish, and even store it. It is necessary to size the food because goldfish of different sizes need food of different sizes. To sort the food, pass the water containing the plankton through two or more sieves

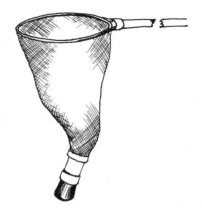

Plankton collecting net

stacked on each other, coarsest on top, finest on the bottom. The smallest plankton organisms will be caught in the lower filter, larger organisms will remain in the top one. Wire mesh sieves can be purchased from biological and specialty aquaculture supply houses, or you can build your own out of gauze netting.

Plankton sorting method using sieves with varying mesh sizes (mesh size decreases from top to bottom).

Growing the Food

In Japan, goldfish breeders cultivate copepods and *Daphnia* in small ponds (20 to 30 square feet or 2 to 3 square meters) in their backyards. They line the bottom of a dry pond with a 2 or 3 inch (5–8 centimeter) layer of pond sludge followed by a ½ inch (about 1–2 centimeter) layer of a mixture of horse and chicken manure. They let this nutrient base rest for several days to mix and dry. They then fill the pond with about 6 to 8 inches (15–20 centimeters) of clean water and inoculate it with rotifers, copepods, and *Daphnia*. When the water temperature reaches 46°F (8°C), the food organisms begin to multiply, although optimum reproduction requires a temperature of 75°–77°F (24°C–25°C). Soon, there is a ready supply of these tiny crustaceans which can be collected every morning with a small strainer.

You may also give your fry other "microfood"—for example, 1-to-2 millimeter-long vinegar eels (*Turbatrix aceti*). They can be cultured easily anywhere. Fill an empty flower pot almost to the brim with coffee grounds slightly moistened with sour milk whey. Do not let the mixture get too wet. Put a small quantity of starter inoculum, obtained from an aquarium lover or pet shop, on this prepared nutrient medium. Add more of the rich sour milk to the surface of the coffee grounds every two or three days, one tablespoon at a time, as it is an excellent food for the vinegar eels. Place a few pebbles the size of marbles in the sour milk and cover the stones with a small glass plate. Then cover the whole flower pot arrangement with a large glass plate. Within a week, the small glass plate on top of the stones will be white with vinegar eels which you can easily scrape off with a knife. You are ready to distribute your "homegrown" food to your young goldfish.

A culture of the extraordinarily nutritious *Enchytraeus,* a white annelid worm resembling a piece of string, is just as easy to grow at home. You need a 16 × 24 × 8 inch (40 × 60 × 20 centimeter) wooden or plastic box. Fill the bottom with a 4 inch (10 centimeter) layer of peat followed by a 2 to 3 inch (5–8 centimeter) layer of humus mixed with a little sand. Then obtain an inoculum of *Enchytraeus* to start your culture. Arrange several heaping teaspoons of rice pudding, oatmeal with milk, or even bread soaked in milk on top of the humus. Cover this "food factory" with a fitted glass plate, and cover the entire culture with a moist cloth. Keep the box in a shaded, rather cool location (54°–64°F, or 12°–18°C) such as a cellar or unheated bathroom, but be careful that the *Enchytraeus* are not attacked by ants (a good way to keep ants away is to suspend the box). After two or three weeks you will have enough worms on the underside of the glass plate to feed your goldfish. Every four or five days the worm food should be replaced to prevent mold.

Brine shrimp (*Artemia salina*), obtainable in most pet shops, can easily be grown at home. If you start with eggs, you can feed the hatching larvae to your goldfish. Or you can raise the brine shrimp to maturity and let them reproduce. Adult brine shrimp are approximately ⅜ inch (1 centimeter) long. Brine shrimp ready to breed will reproduce if kept in a solution of sea salt. Sea salt, which is obtainable at health food stores and many grocery stores, is added to tap water at a concentration of about 1 ounce (30 grams) salt per quart (liter)—the amount need not be at all exact. Add garden fertilizer (*no* weed killer or pesticide) at the concentration recommended on the package. In this nutrient solution, unicellular algae, attached to the shrimp eggs, proliferate rapidly so that the hatching brine shrimp larvae feed on the algae as well as bacteria. You can supplement this food by adding a pinch of yeast per quart to the water. The warmer the water the more quickly the brine shrimp larvae will hatch. At 79°–82°F (26°–28°C) they hatch within 24 hours, and are sexually mature within 14 to 16 days, when they mate and lay new eggs. Keep your brine shrimp cul-

Calico oranda

Diet and Feeding

ture in a warm, sunny spot. Feed adult and late juvenile shrimp to your fish, always leaving a few adults as breeding stock. A coarse fish net will serve to harvest the larger shrimp while leaving the younger ones behind. You will have to add a little fertilizer every two or three weeks to maintain high production of shrimp.

Keeping the Food Fresh

You can keep your supplies of goldfish food fresh in a number of ways. Copepod, *Daphnia,* and insect larvae do best in their original water aerated with a slow stream of large bubbles and kept fairly cool—55°–65°F (12°–18°C). One proven method is to freeze a "jam" of filtered daphnia and copepods. Captured animals are filtered out, placed in a triple plastic bag, and stored in the freezer. The lower the storage temperature the longer the food will keep. Frozen food is particularly useful during the winter because of its high nutrient and vitamin content. To use, break the frozen mixture into pieces the size of walnuts and put them into the water still frozen. Freshly frozen brine shrimp will be readily consumed by the goldfish.

Tubifex worms should be stored in a cool location (about 39°F, or 4°C) inside a china or plastic container covered with a damp cloth. You can keep them just as easily in a bowl or container kept wet by a constant trickle of unchlorinated water.

Dried food may be stored in an airtight jar.

FEEDING METHODS

You can pour live rotifers and *Daphnia* into your goldfish tank in their original water, using a small measuring cup. Insect larvae and whole tubifex worms can be fed to goldfish with tweezers or with your bare hands (always wash your hands afterwards). If you cut up tubifex worms, do so with a sharp knife or razor blade on a cutting board. Wash the cut worms thoroughly in a sieve, spoon the food onto a small plate, and place that on the bottom of the tank. Mix egg yolk mash and commercial fish food with water and pour the mixture onto the carpet of sphagnum moss at the edge of the tank. The small morsels of food cling to this carpet and can easily be discovered by goldfish swimming along the wall.

Goldfish exhibit their normal feeding pattern as soon as the water temperature exceeds 50°F (10°C). As the temperature rises, you can increase the frequency of feeding and the quantity of food. Goldfish's appetite depends on their state of health and on the season. For example, a fish will eat more in the spring than in the fall, even if temperatures are identical. Their appetite is greatest at temperatures of 73°–79°F (23°–26°C). At those temperatures you have to feed juvenile fish three or four times a day and adult fish twice a day. The first feeding should be early in the morning, the last one at dusk. Feed no more than the amount the fish are able to consume within a few minutes (half an hour at the most). Never be too generous, since excess food begins to decay in water within a matter of hours—especially when you are not using live food. Too much food clouds the water and causes the production of toxins, an increase in destructive bacteria, and ultimately the death of fish. It is important always to feed your goldfish at the same location; feed large populations at several spots.

Young fish should consume daily a volume of food approximately equal to the size of their heads. Adults ought to eat 2%–5% of their body weight each day. Rain or a sudden drop in water temperature makes it necessary to reduce this amount of food. If goldfish are hungry, you can train them to come to the water surface near you and to "smack their lips."

TOP: Goldfish and ornamental carp
BOTTOM: Platinum ohgon

GOLDFISH BREEDING

FUNDAMENTALS OF GENETICS

This chapter is intended primarily for those goldfish hobbyists who want not only to keep goldfish but also to breed and raise them as well. To be successful, a goldfish breeder must have a basic understanding of genetics, mainly because the various colors and shapes of today's goldfish varieties were bred according to the principles of heredity.

Goldfish are very "creatable" with respect to certain features and characteristics, and can thus be transformed, to a certain extent at least. This malleability has inherent disadvantages, of course. Goldfish populations can just as easily lose the special colors or veil fins which have been elicited with such great effort. The reason is that the original features of the ancestral wildtype goldfish often emerge to mask the varietal features. The loss of unusual, carefully bred traits indicates the so-called "decline" or "reversion" of a specific variety.

It is a mistake to assume that genetic plasticity—that is, the tendency toward change—involves only external features. Other characteristics are changed to at least the same extent: metabolism, growth rate, life expectancy, and even resistance to disease.

Parents transmit a portion of their characteristic traits to their offspring by way of the male and female reproductive cells. The traits are contained in chromosomes that are in the nuclei of reproductive cells. During division, the reproductive cells of fishes undergo a process called meiosis in which the number of chromosomes, whether in the sperm or in the egg, is halved. A male sperm cell uniting with a female egg cell forms the zygote, which has a chromosome count identical to that of normal body cells.

This number is a constant characteristic of a particular species.

Chromosomes contain the genes (sometimes known as factors) which determine the development or disappearance of a certain characteristic. Genes transmit the hereditary information unique to the particular species and direct the complicated biochemical and cellular processes that occur both during the development of the offspring and its subsequent functioning.

In simple, or Mendelian inheritance, there are two kinds of genes, *dominant* ones (always indicated by capital letters) and *recessive* ones (always indicated by lower case letters). An individual receiving dominant genes from one or both parents will exhibit the dominant character. The recessive character will only emerge if it has been received from both parents. A fish with both dominant or both recessive genes is called "homozygous," whereas a fish with one dominant and one recessive is "heterozygous." If you mate homozygous goldfish of different varieties with one another, you are making a *simple cross*. As an example, if you mate a normal-eyed goldfish with a telescope eye, all offspring (the F_1 generation) will have normal eyes although all will be heterozygous, containing a gene for normal eyes and a gene for telescope eyes. The offspring all exhibit the normal eye because the gene for normal eye is dominant. If you now breed the F_1—remember, each is heterozygous—with each other, offspring with protruding telescope eyes will appear in the next generation (F_2), in a ratio of 3 normal : 1 telescope. This is because some of the offspring of the heterozygous parents ended up with two genes for telescope eyes—two recessive genes. Mendel's Law states that traits segregate in the second (F_2) generation (the "grandchildren") in

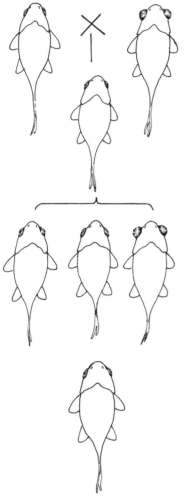

Pattern of heredity for a cross between a telescope eye and a goldfish with normal eyes (after Matsui).

a ratio of 3 : 1 according to dominant and recessive gene pairs.

In intermediate inheritance dominance is lacking. Instead, the two genes interact to produce an intermediate trait in the F_1 generation and an assortment of all three traits in the F_2 generation. For example, one of the characteristic external traits of goldfish is the fin shape. If you cross a long-tailed goldfish (e.g. a veil-tail) with a short-tailed one (e.g. a common domestic goldfish), the offspring in the F_1 generation will have tails of medium length. The next generation (F_2) will include fish with long, medium-length, and short tail fins.

There are some goldfish varieties such as the lionhead and the celestial which are characterized by the absence of a dorsal fin. The offspring, however, even of parents with pure varietal traits and of "purebred" strains, will contain numerous individuals with a normal dorsal fin, a vestigial dorsal fin, or even a humped back. Experience has shown that, in this particular variety, barely 30 percent of the offspring possess the ideal varietal trait (no trace of a dorsal fin). Strict selection and objective evaluation of external appearance is necessary to sustain the characteristic traits of goldfish varieties.

Goldfish color is extremely variable and depends on which chromatic cells are the predominate—black, yellow, red, or white. The different-colored varieties evolve in such a way that one type of chromatic cell becomes dominant while the other colored cells decrease markedly in abundance or even disappear altogether. Pigmentation is due to any or a combination of mutation, selective breeding, cross-breeding different varieties, and the effects of environmental factors.

We should never forget that every type of external shape or color variation is accompanied by internal changes. For example, the resistance to disease of offspring may be considerably lower than that of the parental stock, or the offspring may be sterile as adults. For this reason, a goldfish breeder must exercise discretion to avoid overstepping these "critical limits."

In the course of your breeding efforts, you should, first of all, establish concrete goals and standards for the traits you want to breed. To do this, you have to be fully acquainted with the inheritability of the traits in the fish you are breeding. Remember that your males and females may possess a particular trait to varying degrees, which you will have to take into consideration in every breeding attempt. In any case, your goal should be to raise a large number of offspring to maturity, because only large numbers allow an adequate basis for good selection.

If your first generation of goldfish do not show the desired characteristics, don't despair. Wait until you have bred the F_2 generation, the "grandchildren." The desired results may not appear until then. Breeding new shapes and varieties demands careful work over many years, sometimes decades. But the result, once it is achieved, is worth all the trouble.

GOLDFISH REPRODUCTION

Humans created the goldfish as we know it by means of selective breeding, and the continued existence of goldfish varieties is also closely tied to continuing directed breeding efforts. This means that even the most refined stock will regress when it is neglected—when it reproduces without close supervision and control, and when the offspring mature without selection. Individuals of a neglected breeding stock begin to resemble the original wildtype goldfish after several generations; the progeny merely retain the golden color of their more refined parents.

Reproduction is one of the fundamental biological functions. Breeding, on the other hand, is considerably more defined: it is a method of conscious, directed, controlled reproduction. Breeding plays an especially important role in the reproduction of domesticated animals. In our case, it is responsible for maintaining goldfish varieties.

In the process of fish reproduction, the eggs, except in live-bearing species, are fertilized externally. Therefore, male and female gametes (sperm and egg) unite in the water outside the bodies of the parents. Methods of reproduction resembling the natural process are called spawning. Semi-artificial reproduction (e.g., inducing spawning by means of hormone treatments or preparing artificial nests, in which the females can deposit eggs), although it differs from the normal method, is still characterized as spawning. In artificial reproduction natural spawning does not take place at all. Instead, milt (sperm) and roe (eggs) are taken from the reproductively ripe fish by a method called stripping. After eggs and sperm are mixed, and fertilization has occurred, the resulting zygote cells are allowed to mature and hatch. Hatched larvae are also maintained in an artificial environment. The term "fish breeding" is understood to include not only the measures taken to effect egg fertilization but also to raise fry into their first autumn.

The determination of breeding material, i.e., the selection of males and females, is a basic element of the breeding process, as is rearing goldfish to sexual maturity and preparing them for reproduction.

Sexual Maturation

Whether a goldfish is to be male or female has already been decided in the embryo state. The sex of the fish can only be determined with the naked eye when the fish are yearlings. Male goldfish are sexually mature in their second year. At that age, the oblong, paired, milky-white or faintly pink male gonads (testes) can be seen in the upper portion of the body cavity.

Females become sexually mature in their third year. Their maturation process can be separated into several phases based on ovary development:

In Phase 1, which lasts from hatching to the 18th or 20th month, the female goldfish are still sexually immature. During Phase 1 the ovary can be seen in the upper portion of the body cavity as a thin, pink organ. The so-called "roe structure" of small drops is not yet visible.

Phase 2 characterizes the beginning of the year in which the fish will reach full maturity. In older fish Phase 2 covers the weeks immediately following spawning. The rudimentary ovaries are minute, barely visible balls.

Phase 3 is the period between the 6th and 10th month before spawning, when the developing ovary structures are readily discernible. The still-inactive egg cells are massed together in bundles in the ovary.

Phase 4 covers the weeks just before spawning. The ovary is ready for reproduction—all that is missing now is the right spawning conditions.

In Phase 5, the female goldfish is ready to release her eggs (roe). The individual eggs are completely separated now, and ovarian fluid is the only binding agent holding them in place. Light pressure on the body will eject the eggs, ready to be fertilized.

Good care and diet are indispensible for unimpaired growth and development of goldfish ovaries. Mistakes can lead to deficiencies, which in turn can result in nonsynchronous development and thereby reduce the fertility of the eggs.

The first four phases of ovarian development are largely determined by water temperature. Phase 5 occurs as the result of nerve and hormone activity induced by a suitable spawning environment (temperature, aquatic plants for spawn attachment, presence and courtship of males, and fresh, oxygen-rich water). Phase 4 is actually a state of readiness and waiting. Environmental conditions favorable for spawning during this stage will induce full maturation—that is, Phase 5.

Several features on the goldfish's body indicate that Phase 4 has been reached. In males, nuptial tubercles often appear on the gill coverings; and the stiff rays of the ventral fins display clearly visible, small granular white dots. In the female the large, rounded stomach gets noticeably softer. The total number of eggs which develop in a female goldfish during one spawning season depends on the size of the female and on her care and diet during the previous year. A well-nourished, and hence well-developed, female goldfish 3 years old and 4 to 5 inches (10–12 centimeters) long contains 6,000 to 18,000 eggs. A smaller fish, in its first spawning period produces only 1,000 to 2,000 eggs.

Sexual development of both male and female goldfish is regulated by pituitary hormones. In response to a stimulus from the nervous system the pituitary gland releases a hormone into the blood system. This causes the ovaries to fill up with fluid and the eggs to separate from one another. In this state, the eggs are easily ejected from the body cavity as the female performs the powerful thrashing, rapid turns, and muscle contractions of the spawning ritual.

Spawning

Fertilization takes place in the water outside the bodies of the parent fish. A small appendage with a hole only a few microns wide (the micropyle) forms on the outer cell wall of the egg when it comes in contact with the water. The motile sperm cells traveling in the water penetrate these micropyles to fertilize the egg. The micropyle remains open for only 30 to 60 seconds after the egg is released. If the egg does not get fertilized during this period it is no longer able to accept the sperm cell and fertilization does not take place. The sperm cell is motile only for a short time, as well, usually 1 or 2 minutes. Given these limitations, approximately 30% to 40% of the spawn remains unfertilized. Another cause of non-fertilization can be poor quality gametes, a result of poor care. Even sluggish swimming on the part of either parent during spawning can contribute to reduced fertilization.

Factors that stimulate spawning: The right stimulus to initiate the spawning process may be one or more of various factors, one of the most important being the correct temperature. Goldfish usually spawn in a temperature range of 61°–75°F (16°–25°C), the optimum temperature being 68°F (20°C).

A second stimulus for spawning is fresh, oxygen-rich water that is aged, or "cured," for several days. Under no circumstance should any other fish have been put into the spawning water; any foreign waste products contaminate the water for the mature fish and will prevent them from spawning.

A third factor is a suitable spawning substrate

for the deposition and the attachment of the eggs. Good substrates are finely dissected pondweed or evergreen branches of spruce, juniper, arborvitae, or even root systems or synthetic materials. The feel or "stroking" of a satisfactory substrate indicates to a female that this is the right place to deposit her eggs.

Another decisive factor is the presence of active males driving (chasing) the females. No matter how conducive the environment, without the active participation of males, the females cannot ripen and then spawn. If, with all other factors right, the goldfish still do not spawn, it is usually because the females have not yet reached Phase 4. Another reason may be that the male goldfish do not adequately stimulate the females.

Spawning ritual: Spawning is accompanied by unique movements. First, the males become very excited. In contrast to their usual behavior, they cavort with sudden, quick turns, passing over the aquatic plants of the prospective spawning site so close that the leaves brush against the fishes' bellies. In their frenzy, the males stimulate each other as though one of them were a female. They seem untiring at this point. The females do not yet take part in the ritual. Instead, they withdraw in apparent intimidation to a far corner of the aquarium. But their inactivity is deceptive for, although you do not really notice anything in their movement, the females are in one of the most intensely active phases of their life. They observe the males' ritual for some time. The most precocious males begin to chase the females in order to drive chosen ones toward the aquatic plants for spawning. But normally, the males do not succeed at this point. This unusual activity on the part of the males, their attempts to drive the females, and the females' recognition of the spawning site precipitate a transformation in the female goldfish. Their taut stomachs become suddenly soft, and they lose all trace of the listlessness typical of the previous weeks. They be-

come drawn toward the cavorting males. All of a sudden, one of the females takes off in the direction of the spawning site, the males rush towards to her, dance around her nudging her stomach with their heads, and try to drive her to the spawning site. Arriving at the right spot, the female makes one or two quick turns, then suddenly freezes, and releases a few eggs. Meanwhile, the male goldfish begin to display, and inject milt (sperm) into the water among the eggs. At intervals they chase the female around in order to induce further egg releases.

Spawning continues for several hours, with occasional short interruptions. More females enter the scene and, ultimately, all of the goldfish display and dance above the plants. From time to time, some of the females will take a break and then return to the group. The ritual dance that accompanies spawning gradually subsides until, towards the end of mating, the males are driving only one or two of the females. Finally, all female goldfish leave the mating site. They are exhausted now, and lie on the bottom of the tank without stirring. No matter how active a male might be now, it could not induce a female to start swimming again.

In most females the eggs mature sequentially. After spawning her first set of eggs, a female will usually spawn again in a few weeks. Some goldfish even spawn as late as early fall.

Embryo Development

After spawning the eggs, which are small, yellow-white spheres, dot the leaves of aquatic plants. Their diameter is 1 to 1.5 millimeters (about $\frac{1}{32}$ inch). At the time of spawning the eggs are considerably smaller but they triple their volume upon coming in contact with water. They absorb water, causing the outer layer to expand while the ovum enclosed by the inner layer is suspended in the interior of the egg, known as the perivitelline space.

The development of fertilized eggs, also called incubation, can be divided into four phases:

1. fertilization and expansion of the ovum,

Goldfish Breeding

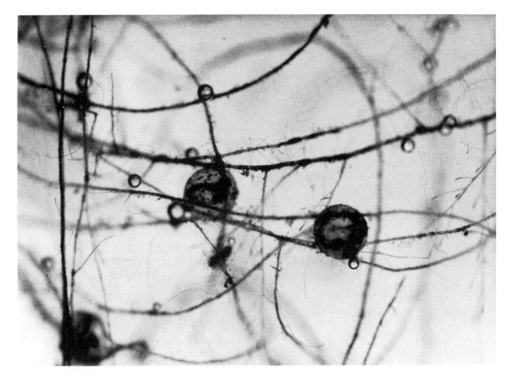

Goldfish eggs attached to filamentous algae

2. germ layer (blastula) development,
3. embryo development, and
4. pre-larval stage.

Within each of these four stages, development can again be subdivided into typical substages. These substages are listed in Table 6.

The duration of the embryonic period depends on temperature. Goldfish eggs can develop normally in a temperature range of 54°–81°F (12°–27°C), although, of course, development is slower at temperatures below 68°F (20°C). Temperatures outside the normal range can cause an increase in the number of fish which will die in their eggs or before being able to feed themselves. At optimum incubation temperatures (64°–72°F, or 18°–22°C), the fish hatch in 4 or 5 days as Table 7 shows.

There are always a number of eggs which do not get fertilized. Initially, they look the same, even under a microscope, as fertilized spawn.

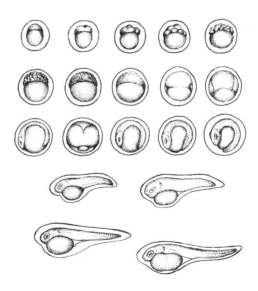

Embryonic development of goldfish

Table 6. Developmental Stages of Goldfish Eggs

Stage	Substage	Characteristics
Fertilization		
	1. Pre-fertilization	The egg coating surrounds the ovule (immature egg cell).
	2. Fertilization	The small aperture (micropyle) for a sperm cell to enter the ovule develops, and the eggs swell in volume.
	3. Ovum phase	The ovum structure changes, it separates into two distinct parts: an opaline (animal) part with dividing cells and a transparent (vegetative) nutritive part. Separation of the egg coating from the ovum is already apparent.
Germ Layer Development		
	4. Cell division	The opaline cell part divides into two cells which continue the process of doubling by cell division.
	5. Morular stage	The part with dividing cells changes into a mulberry-shaped structure called the morula (Latin: *morulus* = deep black, mulberry).
	6. Blastula	The cell structure of the living animal part changes completely. The cells (micromeres) now sit atop the spherical nutritive blastocoele (yolk).
	7. Late blastula	The blastula flattens and spreads out over the yolk.
Embryo Development		
	8. Gastrulation (pear stage)	Due to invagination of the blastoderm, consisting of the dividing cells, the embryo becomes pear-shaped.
	9. Head development	The embryo entirely surrounds the yolk sac on one side, and an elongation marking the head is noticeable.
	10. Eye and vertebral development	The contours of the eye become visible, as does the structure of the vertebrae in the backbone.
	11. Tail development	The tail detaches from the yolk sac.
	12. Tail growth	The tail gets longer.
	13. Eyed-egg stage	Eye pigmentation; the iris in the eyes turn black.
Pre-larval Stage		The fish moves actively in the egg and will soon hatch.

Later, the inner portion of unfertilized eggs turns cloudy and the egg becomes covered with fungus. This is dangerous because the fungus-infested eggs may contaminate nearby fertilized eggs, killing the embryos by depleting their oxygen. If the percentage of unfertilized eggs is high, the fungus can take over, contaminating all fertilized eggs. Preventive measures are described in the chapter on fish diseases.

TOP: Kawa Goi, a white-yellow ornamental carp without scales
BOTTOM: Gimbo

Table 7. Maturation Times for Goldfish Eggs at Various Incubation Temperatures

Water temperature (°F / °C)	Incubation time (days)
54 / 12	15
57 / 14	10
63 / 17	7
66 / 19	5
70 / 21	4
73 / 23	3.5
77 / 25	3
81 / 27	2.5

Larval and Fry Stages

During the last stage of an egg's development, the pre-larva is ready to hatch and to begin to live independently. When temperature and oxygen conditions are ideal the larva makes no effort to leave the egg. In unfavorable conditions, however, the larva may hatch before it is fully developed. Prematurely hatching young fish reveal their debility by their behavior. Most do not attach themselves to plants or to the aquarium walls but instead lie on the bottom of the tank. The whole brood of premature larvae makes no attempt to adhere to a substratum until the following day.

Hatching is normally induced by oxygen depletion even in the best of conditions. The goldfish has developed until the narrow confines of the egg no longer afford it enough space, oxygen, or movement. The larva begins to produce an enzyme which dissolves the egg's outer membrane, allowing the goldfish to free itself. The newly hatched larva makes forceful swimming motions and promptly adheres to plants or tank walls in order to escape the danger of perishing from the low and irregular oxygen supply of the bottom. Recently hatched larvae 5 or 6 millimeters long remain attached for two to four days, depending on the temperature. They move very little during this time, nourished by their yolk sac. Do not disturb the larvae at this point. Should their substratum, or the surrounding water, move, they become detached and expend energy unnecessarily to find a new attachment site.

Too much light or a significant drop in temperature are also injurious to these tiny fish. For that reason, cover the aquarium from midday sun and cool nights to protect it.

The end of the larval stage is near when the larvae try to swim horizontally, leaving their suspended attachment sites more and more often. Then they begin to swim to the water surface for oxygen, and this is really the point at which the larvae become functioning fish. They inflate their swim bladders with air, and are now finally capable of swimming horizontally for longer periods.

The small goldfish (now fry) begin to breathe through their gills and to feed on their own. Their natural food consists of minute algae, rotifers, and copepod larvae. It is very important to provide adequately shredded food (0.05 to 0.1 millimeter long) during this time. If the small fry cannot find suitable food they become weak, and many of them perish. Ample feeding is essential for the initial good health of fry and is an important factor both for good development of individual varietal characteristics and for proper later development.

HOW TO BREED GOLDFISH THROUGH SPAWNING

Selection and Care of Breeding Stock

Selection of breeding stock begins when the fish are still very young. Your goldfish stock should consist of perfect, exquisite representatives of the particular variety. Fish which have lived under ideal conditions continuously and

TOP: Kin Kabuto
BOTTOM: Koshino Hisoku

have been able to develop well because of appropriate nourishment form a good foundation for breeding crosses. Yearling fish should be at least 2 to 2½ inches (5–6 centimeters) long—about as long as a chicken egg. Two-year-old individuals should exceed 3 inches (8–9 centimeters), three-year-olds should be about 4½ inches (11–12 centimeters) long. Flawed individuals or those susceptible to disease should not be used for breeding. Use male goldfish more than two years old and females over three years old. Although goldfish a year or so younger than this are capable of breeding, reproduction with them is always unpredictable.

During the year before breeding you should pay special attention to your goldfish. Offer them a wide variety of high-quality foods (*Daphnia*, tubifex worms, soya grits, alfalfa mash or meal, fresh ground meat, special commercial fish foods, and so forth). Take care to provide the fish with the best possible overwintering conditions, and to transfer them to a sunny tank as soon in the spring as possible. At this time—if they are able to feed themselves—give them fresh, live food whenever possible. But do not overfeed them. Fat fish cannot be expected to produce perfect offspring, and a large number of their offspring

will not be viable. Depending on the weather, young goldfish destined to be breeding stock should be separated by sex at the beginning or, at the very latest, by the end of April. Use the sexual characteristics of goldfish listed in Table 8 to separate the fish.

Check the segregated stock several times to make absolutely sure that no fish of one sex remains with fish of the other sex. It often happens that individual goldfish do not exhibit their sexual characteristics until just before spawning, so that it is very easy to place them in the wrong group. You have to remove these fish immediately because they may induce premature spawning and could thus ruin your whole breeding schedule. Normally in such instances several fish spawn prematurely while the other fish eat the spawn. Premature spawning usually occurs among the best-conditioned individuals, which results in losing the controlled spawn of your choicest specimens.

Continue to feed the brood you segregated by sex. Treat the fish against parasites as needed (see under "Diseases"). Change the water only when absolutely necessary up until the end of the spawning period, this will cause the fish to feel much more comfortable when they are

Table 8. Sexual Dimorphism in Goldfish

Criterion	Female	Male
body shape	round, thickset	angular, slender
abdominal wall	roundish, soft prior to mating	flat, hard
anal pore*	double, protruding and red prior to mating	single; prior to mating, white milt may be released by stroking
anal fin**	thin, smooth	thick, dotted white prior to mating
pectoral fin**	smooth even prior to mating	dotted white prior to mating, nuptial tubercles on the thickest fin ray
gill cover (operculum)	smooth	dotted white prior to mating, white nuptial tubercles on the back ray

Note: * see illustration on page 79
    **see illustration on page 79

transferred to the breeding tanks. There, the fresh, clean water acts as a stimulant, encouraging spawning. It is preferable to let algae grow enough to turn the water in the separate tanks a light green. These conditions provide an ideal environment for breeding fish prior to spawning. Should the water from one tank flow into the other tank, place the females in the tank which gets the fresh water first. The reason is that the presence of waste products from male fish in the females' water has a disruptive effect on the sexual maturation of the females.

Nuptial tubercles (or pearl organs) on the anterior part of the pectoral fins and on the operculum of a male goldfish

The beginning of spawning can be ascertained by careful observation of the breeding stock. It is signaled by the appearance of white dots (nuptial tubercles) on the gill flaps and ventral fins of the males, by the gravid, rounded and softening bellies of the females, and by the appearance of a pinkish protuberance on the anal pore of some fish ("spawning spine"). The majority of fish will develop these characteristics when the water temperature remains constant in the range 61°–66°F (16°–19°C), usually at the end of April or beginning of May.

Mating

Start mating your goldfish when your stock is ripe for spawning. At first, try mating one or two of your less exquisite females. If you succeed, then let your prize individuals mate. You may mate the goldfish in pairs, in small or large breeding sets, or as a group. A small breeding set consists of one female and two to three males, while a large breeding set has two females and three males. For group mating, in which several small breeding sets reproduce together, place two males into the spawning tank for every female. Natural mating calls for more males than females because the fish move so fast during spawning that often the milt does not come in contact with the roe.

Anal pores of male and female goldfish

Preparing the tank and nest The best choice for a mating location is an outdoor tank, but the fish will also reproduce in larger indoor aquariums. To mate pairs or small breeding sets, you need a surface area of approximately 10 square feet (1 square meter). For large breeding sets, you need 15 square feet (1.5 square meters). You'll need 15 to 20 square feet (1.5–2 square meters) of surface area for each female and accompanying two males when you group breed the fish. The optimum water depth for mating is approximately 6 inches (15 centimeters).

Start your preparations with a thorough

cleaning of the breeding tank, including careful washing, disinfection, and repeated rinsing. Then check the drain and test whether it is truly watertight. This is crucial because freshly-hatched goldfish can be swept away through a crack only 0.3 millimeters wide.

The next step is to fill the clean tank with aged, clean, oxygen-rich water as close to 68°F (20°C) as possible. After filling the tank, place the spawning substrate in the center of the tank. This support substrate may be an aquatic plant, an evergreen branch, a willow or alder root, or even the now popular synthetic materials. Of the available aquatic plants, water milfoil and *Elodea* are most suitable. False cypress, juniper, or spruce are the best conifers. The best synthetic structures are usually imitations of these plants. The most practical way to assemble a spawning nest is to tie all the materials comprising the nest to a rustfree, non-corrosive ring, weighing the ring down if necessary to ensure that the nest rests securely on the bottom of the tank.

A spawning nest assembled from aquatic plants

The diameter of the nest should be 12 to 16 inches (30–40 centimeters), its height about 2½ to 3 inches (6–8 centimeters). The nest must be arranged in such a way that the ejected spawn will be distributed over its entire height and breadth. If the nest is too shallow the eggs are apt to stick to each other, resulting in suffocation of eggs located below. Make sure that the nest is bushy and extends a few inches/centimeters above the bottom of the tank. By the same token, a nest too high is also a disadvantage because spawning fish cannot easily swim back and forth over the nest, so that a large percentage of the spawn falls to the bottom of the tank around the nest. When planning your nests, make one nest per pair or small breeding set, two nests for each large breeding set, and one nest per female for group mating.

Once the nests are placed in the tank, all that remains to be done is to cover the tank to provide shade and to prevent rapid cooling. Now everything is ready to go.

Releasing the fish The next step is to release the fish. The best time is early afternoon. Take special care to be gentle when capturing your fish and placing them in the tank. Rough handling can spoil all your efforts, because goldfish will not mate when they have been injured. Release the fish into the water just above the nests so that they will immediately see the plant structures intended for spawning.

Given healthy, breeding individuals and good weather, mating may take place as early as the next morning. Normally, goldfish placed in a breeding tank will mate within one or two days. Mating usually lasts from sunrise until early afternoon. The process does not end until all females have finally left the nest area.

Separating the spawn At this stage, spawn and goldfish must be separated or the adults will eat most of their spawn. The usual practice is to remove the fish from the breeding tank but you may also transfer the nest to another similarly prepared tank for the development of the spawn. It is preferable, however, to transfer the fish. This gives the spawn which fell to the bottom near the nest a chance to mature, as well. When you remove the adult goldfish, take into consideration that the females may spawn again in another 10 to 12 days. Therefore, the mating pair or breeding set should still be kept in separate tanks. Following mating, feed the goldfish with ample live food. You may also find it worthwhile to put a sample of the spawn in a small jar or aquarium in order to determine the fertility rate and the expected incubation time. The sample container should be maintained at 73° to 77°F (23°–25°C) and should be supplied with sufficient oxygen by adding several aquatic plants or an aerator. In this way, you can advance the hatching time of the spawn sample and thereby estimate the number of larvae you will be getting in your outside tank.

Encouraging Egg Development

Successful mating and spawning is by no means synonymous with complete breeding success. The spawn must also be protected and cared for. It is essential to avoid precipitous temperature changes. As we mentioned earlier, the optimum spawning temperature is 68°F (20°C). You should always ensure that the tank temperature does not deviate from this average by more than 4°F (2°C). Japanese scientists have discovered that at temperatures below 59°F (15°C) or above 79°F (26°C) the number of young fish born with developmental defects increases greatly. Caudal fin defects, in particular, occur much more frequently. To prevent excessive heating, provide shading for the spawning tank. Prevent excessive cooling by covering the tank at night.

In addition to the temperature, pay attention to the freshness, cleanliness, and oxygen content of the water. Cloudy water in the spawning tank is a sign of invasive growth of bacteria, rotifers, or both. Should this happen, transfer the nest with the spawn to a clean tank and disinfect the old one. Cloudiness causes temporary oxygen deficiency which may suffocate the spawn. In minor cases of clouding, a partial water change, aeration, or even filtration is all that is needed.

Make sure that the water temperature remains constant when you are trying these options.

Protection from the growth of fungus on dead eggs is also very important. A preventive measure consists of dipping the nests into a malachite green solution with a concentration of 10 parts per million. Such a bath should only take place if a large portion of the spawn (40%–60%) is infected.

Hatching

Hatching is near when the eyes of the embryos in the eggs darken, an indication of the formation of pigment cells. The spawn is called "eyed eggs" at this phase, and have successfully completed 70 to 80 percent of their incubation time.

The initiation of hatching can be recognized by the fact that several larvae are hanging from the nest branches or on the tank wall. Goldfish hatching may last from half a day to a day, depending on the temperature. Remove the nests only after all living eggs have hatched. If the nest is made of non-perishable materials, it can be reused after it has been disinfected. Use the same solutions for disinfection as you would for the tank. In place of the removed nests, provide new opportunities for the larval fish to attach themselves. If larvae are numerous, attachment surfaces made of synthetic fibers, e.g., mosquito netting stretched over a plastic frame, have proven to be very practical. If a large device is needed, tree branches or wood are unsuitable because they create an oxygen deficiency in the tank at night. Like spawn, the larvae must be protected from strong sunlight, heat, and cold. Copepods are unwelcome guests in a spawning tank. Should any multiply from windborne eggs you can kill them with a 1 ppm solution of trichlorophon. This concentration is not harmful to larvae.

The larval stage ends when the tiny goldfish start swimming and feeding on their own. From that point on the fish (now fry) are less sensitive to light and temperature variations.

Goldfish

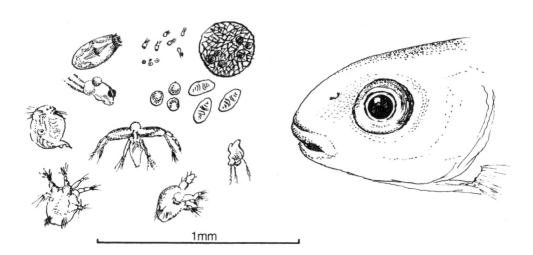

Relative size of a goldfish fingerling and the organisms comprising its diet

Feeding the Fry

When goldfish begin to swim horizontally, they also begin to seek external food sources. Traces of the yolk sac remain, but the bulk of the organism's energy requirement comes from external sources. Asian goldfish breeders feed their fry boiled egg yolk mixed with water. Boiled egg yolk breaks up into very small particles which even fry can consume. But again, don't overfeed. Egg yolk spoils very rapidly and pollutes the water. That is a considerable problem in tanks containing fry because it is very difficult to change the water or to catch and transfer the tiny fish. To prevent too much food or oversized food particles from getting into the water, press the yolk mixture through a very fine strainer. Excellent types of live food valuable for raising fry are tiny rotifers and the nauplius larvae of copepods. Adult copepods must not get into the tank during the first seven to ten days, i.e., during the initial stage of feeding.

Fry more than ten days old may be fed larger crustaceans. The major sources of food should now be young *Daphnia* and *Cyclops*. You may begin serving finely-chopped tubifex worms and finely-ground soy meal, commercial fish food specifically for fry, and cream of wheat. Be sparing in your use of enriched foods since overfeeding tends to fatten the goldfish, and your young fish could easily become "soft" and flabby.

Feed fry two to three weeks old what you feed older goldfish.

Selection of Young Fish

Even the offspring of the most prized parent goldfish will occasionally contain individuals not exhibiting the characteristic features of their particular variety, but instead resembling the wildtype goldfish. It goes without saying that such individuals must be excluded from the breeding process. This is not just a matter of aesthetics. It is necessary primarily because these individuals are usually much hardier. They are superior swimmers and mature much more rapidly than their varietal siblings. The difference in growth rate can even lead to cannibalism, and the victims will be your choicest breeding examples because the varietal characteristics are most pronounced in them. One major task of selection, therefore, is to cull those young fish which resemble the original wildtype. The first selection takes place when the fry are ⅜ to ⅝ inch (1–1.5 centimeters) long, i.e., about the 14th to 20th day after hatching.

The selection procedure is as follows: First, lower the water level by draining to simplify catching the fish. Remember to cover the siphon hose or the drain with fine gauze, or place the hose inside a screened box (see illustration on p. 83). The fry congregating at the bottom of the tank can be taken out with a flat ladle. A

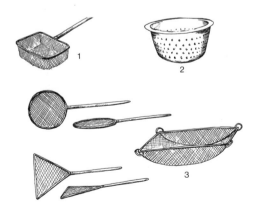

Box screen with rubber hose for siphoning water from tanks holding fry.

Glass pipe for removing fingerlings

Equipment for raising fry: 1) bulging and shallow nets, 2) holding basket, 3) holding net

fish net is not recommended since the fish may become too dry and die. Transfer the tiny fish to plastic buckets and then remove them individually with the aid of an enamel or plastic ladle and examine the shape of the caudal fin. Individuals characterized by a double or multi-sectioned caudal fin already show the rudiments of the horizontal, laterally positioned fin. Goldfish with simple caudal fins do not yet have this widening tail base. They are the ones that must be removed from the other fish. During this first selection process, take a count of the offspring in order to evaluate the results of spawning and incubation.

After cleaning the tank, return the selected fish to the tank. Continue to keep an eye out for noticeably larger individuals that are snatching the best morsels of food away from the others and are, consequently, growing more rapidly. Remove such fish from the tank but do not exclude them from the breeding program if they have the desired features—just keep them separate.

The next selection should take place a month later, when the fish are six to eight weeks old. This time, examine the caudal fin development closely, paying special attention to whether all corresponding lobes are of similar shape and size. Cull individuals with differently shaped or sized fins.

At this time, you can also begin to recognize the dorsal fin. If lack of a dorsal fin is characteristic of the variety in question, cull all individuals with dorsal fins or vestiges of dorsal fins. Individuals with crooked or deformed backs and with misshapen fins are also unsuitable. The fact that coloration or other special characteristics may not yet have developed in some individuals is not a reason for exclusion at this time.

Carry out the third selection process when the stock is one year old, right after its first winter. At this time, characteristic shapes, coloration, and scale arrangement of individual varieties are developed and clearly visible. Defects are also apparent—hunched backs, excessively long peduncles, vestigial dorsal fins, and so forth. After this selection, only the most attractive individuals will remain in your stock. You can now assume that individuals of the different varieties will develop properly and will resemble the type fish of the given variety. At three years of age, all traits are fully developed.

Selection should still continue, however. Although your stock will be further reduced, the decrease in quantity will be offset by an increase in quality. Details of the different selection criteria for individual varieties would be outside the scope of this book. Let your selection process be guided by the illustrations and photographs provided. Asian goldfish breeders maintain that the art of selection can be mastered only after long personal experience—we would not presume to refute this centuries' old maxim with a catalogue of rules.

HOW TO BREED GOLDFISH ARTIFICIALLY

As the result of research over the last 80 years, fishes that play an important role in human nutrition are now being bred artificially. The process was first perfected for trout species. Then artificial breeding was developed for pike and whitefish, and carp. Because goldfish are closely related to carp, they can be bred in a similar way.

The simple method of artificial fertilization of carp entails removing a ripe female from the tank, drying her off, and stripping the eggs carefully into a small porcelain or plastic bowl. For stripping, press your fingers lightly against both sides of the female's abdomen, stroking it in the direction of the genital pore. Under no circumstance should the spawn come into contact with water; for that reason, fish and bowl must both be dry. Strip one or several males of milt (sperm) in the same fashion. Mix the eggs and sperm together and then add water. Use a horn spoon, glass rod, or a feather for mixing.

The fertilized eggs are placed in a glass tank to mature until hatching. In our opinion, the method is very successful: a single pair of goldfish can produce up to 10,000 offspring.

Artificial breeding of goldfish as developed from this method of artificial carp breeding is somewhat more complicated, but it is even more successful. Because the time of natural mating is uncertain, the probability of finding a "ripe" pair at just the right moment is relatively small. And if you do, that particular pair may already have mated anyway.

Administering Hormones

In order to control the time at which the fish can be stripped the common practice of administering hormones is now recommended for the production of commercial fish. Basically, the method consists of injecting a pituitary gland extract into the dorsal muscles, directly above the ventral fin and between the dorsal and lateral lines of the goldfish intended for stripping. This extract can be obtained from suppliers to the fish breeding industry. The first step is to calculate the dosage according to the weight of the fish. The recommended dosage for female fish is 0.3 milligrams of dried pituitary extract per 100 grams (3.5 ounces) of body weight. A small pellet of pituitary extract weighs 2 to 3 milligrams, enough for 700 to 1000 grams (approximately 1½ to 2 pounds) of female goldfish.

The weight of well-developed females ranges from 80 to 120 grams (approx. 3–4 ounces). Therefore, each fish should receive about 0.25 to 0.36 milligrams of pituitary extract. The preparation is administered in a 0.9% salt solution ("physiological or normal saline," available in ampules from drug stores). The dried pituitary extract is finely ground in a porcelain mortar and mixed into the saline solution. Then the correct amount of solution to inject is calculated. For example, if you mix 4 milligrams

TOP: Kagami Goi
BOTTOM: Kohaku

of pituitary extract in 2 milliliters of saline solution and your fish weighs 120 grams you inject it with 0.2 milliliters of solution. That amount of solution contains 0.4 milligrams of extract. Although the exact dose should be 0.36 milligrams, we always round off to the next higher tenth of a milligram because it is impractical to inject precise amounts into goldfish and it is necessary to make an allowance for spillage. To administer the dose use a 1 cc (= ml) syringe graduated in $\frac{1}{100}$ cc and a #19 or #20 needle with a 0.2 millimeter interior diameter.

Insert the needle under the scales and into the back muscle. After injecting the dose, and with the needle still in place, stroke lightly over the injection site.

Males receive 0.1 milligram pituitary extract for each 100 grams of body weight, administered in the same fashion as for the females.

Stripping and Fertilizing

The stripping process of the artificial and natural methods are almost identical. The only difference is that you do not initiate fertilization in water, but in a Woynarovich solution (1 liter water, 4 grams non-iodized table salt, and 3 grams urea). Dilute the roe and milt, which have been dry, with this solution, adding only a little at first and mixing it immediately with the entire spawn. The advantage of this solution is that it not only activates the sperm but also makes the eggs less sticky. This simplifies their handling and assures their fertilization and thus maturation.

Continue stirring the eggs in this solution for a few minutes. Fertilization actually occurs within the first minute; additional stirring prevents the eggs from adhering to one other. Then add five or six times the original amount of solution to the spawn mixture and let it stand for an hour, stirring every eight to ten minutes. To eliminate egg stickiness completely, you will need

TOP: Tancho Kohaku
BOTTOM: Shiro Bekko

still another solution composed of 1.5 grams tannic acid dissolved in 1 liter of water. After draining the first solution, place the eggs in this second solution for no more than ten seconds. Then rinse well with clean water. All solutions and rinses should be at the same temperature. The final step is to bathe the eggs in a weak solution of tannic acid (0.3 mg per liter of water) for 30 to 60 seconds and rinsing with clean pond water. Now, at last, the development of the eggs can take its course.

Caring for the Eggs and Larvae

You can incubate your eggs on a large scale in small fish incubators called Zug bottles. If you are only working with a few thousand eggs, however, you can use a swimming frame covered with gauze (0.5 millimeter mesh size). Be sure that there is only a single layer of spawn on the gauze. The course of development of artificially-fertilized spawn is identical to that of spawn deposited under natural conditions.

Even using the Zug bottle method, the eggs hatch on a swimming frame. As soon as they reach the stage of eyed eggs and a few larvae have hatched, the eggs are transferred to the frame. Sunlight and the slightly warmer water will accelerate hatching. The optimum temperature for hatching is 73° to 75°F (23–24°C). When all larvae have left the eggs, you can place them in the same tank that held the frames. Provide enough attachment sites for the larvae, as described previously. Larvae and fry hatched from artificially fertilized eggs are treated in the same manner as those produced by natural mating and spawning.

Advantages of Artificial Breeding

At first glance, artificial reproduction seems to be considerably more complicated than natural spawning. In fact, you are probably wondering why this method is even necessary. Would it not be easier to stay with the original method? To be honest, we must agree that artificial breeding does indeed demand more practice and more work. It is, therefore, recommended only for those goldfish lovers who are seriously interested in breeding and refining goldfish. For those breeders, this method is very important, however, since it is more productive and effective than natural spawning, guaranteeing the fertilization of a much greater portion of each female's eggs. The average percentage of infertile eggs in natural spawning is 40%–50%. Artificial reproduction can lower this figure to below 10%.

In addition, remember that several males mate with one female in natural reproduction while in artificial breeding the eggs of any one female are fertilized by a single male. From a genetic point of view, this is a major consideration for breeding goldfish whose volatile varietal characteristics are difficult to consolidate and perpetuate.

ANNUAL SCHEDULE OF GOLDFISH CARE

January and February: This is the coldest time of year. It is crucial to keep cold-sensitive varieties, such as lionheads and black telescope eyes at relatively warm temperatures (57°–61°F; 14°–16°C). You have several options. Adult goldfish are content with shaded, weakly lighted cement tanks, plastic or wooden containers, or aquariums. Younger fish, of about seven or eight months, however, require an aquarium or a bright tank, preferably exposed to sunlight, and a temperature of 64°–68°F (18°–20°C). These conditions are preconditions for the continued development of the fish. Incidentally, unicellular algae which give the water a green color also multiply very quickly under these conditions, a favorable by-product. Change the water once a week with aged but clean water of the same temperature. Yearling fish should be fed twice a day, adult individuals just once.

Simpler varieties, such as common domestic goldfish and orandas, may be kept in outdoor tanks during the winter. See the section on overwintering for the care and feeding of fish overwintering outdoors. Fish hibernating outdoors do not need to be fed; therefore, their water does not need to be changed. Check the general behavior and health of your goldfish every week or two through the window or by removing the tank cover.

March: The weather may still be cold in March. Consequently, continue to keep the more delicate goldfish varieties warm.

This is the time to start increasing the number of feedings and the quantity of food per feeding. Provide diversity in your goldfish's diet by including copepods, *Daphnia,* tubifex worms, and other items.

As soon as the danger of night frost has passed, the leaf lattice may be removed from outdoor tanks, especially during the second half of the month. A few days later, start removing the boards and tarpaper layer by layer. Replace this cover in very cold nights. During the day, remove the sludge and detritus accumulated on the tank bottom by siphoning and change the tank water with water of the same temperature. When the water temperature reaches 48°–50°F (9°–10°C) try to start feeding your fish. Be careful and feed only small amounts which the fish can consume within a few minutes.

April: April weather is notoriously unpredictable. Be prepared to protect your fish during cold snaps.

This month marks the beginning of breeding preparations. The goldfish marked as breeding stock must now be fed larger quantities of a varied diet. The sexes should be separated and carefully prepared for mating. As a safety measure, disinfect the tanks again as you did in the fall.

Fill the spawning tanks with fresh water during the second half of April. As soon as the temperature rises above 61°F (16°C), you may transfer the fish to breeding tanks, including three males for every female. Under favorable conditions of temperature, the goldfish may be ready to mate by the end of the month.

If the water gets too cold, velvet disease (costiasis) is apt to crop up. For that reason, observe the skin and fins of your goldfish carefully on a daily basis and check for any evidence of a yellowish, silky-matte coating.

For fish kept in ornamental ponds, your only concern is proper feeding, health checks, and continuous general checks.

Goldfish

May: If April was not yet conducive to mating, your fish will in all likelihood breed early in May.

The goldfish are very vigorous and active during this period. Adult fish must be fed three times a day, young fish as often as four times a day.

Change the water every five days in a ratio of 3 : 1—3 gallons of fresh, aged water to 1 gallon of old water left in the tank.

Goldfish breeders work hardest at this time: frequent feedings, breeding, care of the young, cleaning, and changing water. But this is also the most rewarding time. For us, it has always been the best time of the whole year.

June: By now, all your goldfish have mated. One of the most important tasks following mating is the health care of your valuable breeding stock. Check for injuries and unusual weakness. It is time, too, to transfer the fish to another tank. Food should be rationed somewhat; the fish need less food than during the pre-breeding period, or they will gain too much weight and skip the next breeding season.

Young goldfish hatched in late April or early May are about the size of pumpkin seeds at this point. Pay attention to the number of fry per square foot of tank space.

If June is cold and rainy, the tanks should be covered at night. If the month is hot, provide the tanks with shading. Change one third of the water every four or five days.

Sphagnum moss and filamentous algae tend to get the upper hand in the tanks holding your fry. Try to avoid that condition because the small fish can perish in the profuse vegetation.

Finally, begin the first selection of young fish during June.

July: In moderate climates, you have to worry less about cold nights than about hot days. Whenever the water temperature reaches 77°F (25°C), you absolutely must shade approximately 70% to 80% of the water surface of the

tanks holding your fry. For adult fish, 50% of the water surface should be shaded. Increase shading with increasing temperatures. At the same time, you can cool down the water temperature during the hottest hours of the day by adding cooled, aged water to the tank. Check that tank water does not get contaminated by a buildup of dead algae. Such deterioration of the water quality can lead to oxygen depletion and a buildup of toxins, poisoning your fish. This is one of the main reasons for the relatively frequent water changes, usually every four or five days.

Under favorable conditions, the colors of the young fish will now change to the adult pattern. Pigmentation changes are greatly promoted by early morning sun when the sun's full light hits the water surface at an angle. These color changes tend to make the goldfish listless and weak which, in turn, slows their growth temporarily. Therefore, reduce the quantity of food and change the water only every eight to ten days.

The adult body conformation of fish of excellent "lineage" take shape during this period.

After the fish have changed color, transfer them to a tank with at least 7 or 8 inches (18–20 centimeters) of water. The water should be changed every four or five days again.

Young goldfish must be fed generously; breeding or ornamental fish need only moderate feedings.

August: Continue feeding the fish and shading and changing the water as in July. Be sure to provide enough shade, since the "cap" of the lionhead, and other head embellishments, will shrivel under intense sun. Too much exposure to sun can also cause color changes in goldfish.

In late August the weather starts changing, in moderate climates at least, bringing thunderstorms and rain. Air and water may start to cool off. Should the water temperatures fall below 64°–68°F (18°–20°C), cover the tanks at night, particularly those tanks holding temperature-sensitive varieties. In the event of heavy downpours, make certain that the tanks do not flood—your goldfish could easily spill over the tank edge.

September: Long experience has shown that weather during the first half of September is much like that during late August. Therefore, the care of your goldfish continues as before.

If the weather turns warmer for an Indian summer, you can increase your goldfish's food again and change the water every six to eight days. Cold nights require covering the tanks holding young fish or temperature-sensitive varieties.

In Japan, late September is the time for goldfish exhibitions and contests which feature not only the mature breeding fish but also the offspring of the current year. This ancient tradition, imitated in many countries, is instructive and entertaining for breeders and hobbyists alike.

October: Although October often gives us warm, sunny days, there is no doubt that fall has definitely arrived.

Remove any shading devices from the tank during the day but replace them at night to prevent the water from cooling off too much.

If the water temperature does not exceed 55°–59°F (13°–15°C) during the day, reduce the amount of food. In October goldfish rely heavily on green algae. Provide them with filamentous algae and "green" water to promote the development of final skin pigmentation, a beautiful sheen to the scales, and resistance to disease.

You do not yet have to worry about hardy goldfish or those living in garden ponds. They merely get less food—about as much as they can consume in 15 to 20 minutes.

The last days of October are the time to start preparations for the overwintering process which is the key to success of next year's breeding season.

Set up winter aquariums and tanks for temperature-sensitive fish, i.e. for those which need temperatures no lower than 57°–61°F (14°–16°C).

As soon as outdoor temperatures fall below 50°F (10°C), begin to transfer the temperature-sensitive goldfish varieties indoors and disinfect their tanks. Before placing the fish into their winter quarters, however, treat them for parasites. Then your goldfish can begin their overwintering phase in a healthy condition.

November: As soon as the first frost appears, remove the mud from the tanks of the hardier goldfish varieties and cover the tanks for the winter. You can really help your fish now by bubbling air into the tank with the aid of an aquarium air pump. The air bubbles will prevent the formation of ice. Hardier goldfish can even spend the winter under a cover of ice if the water depth is at least 8 inches (20 centimeters). But you must keep air holes open at all times.

The health of temperature-sensitive as well as hardy goldfish varieties should be checked every week or two. In the winter the fish are highly susceptible to velvet disease, which can crop up overnight.

Goldfish overwintering outdoors do not need to be fed. Other goldfish receive only sparing amounts of food.

December: In mild temperatures above freezing, you may remove part of the tank covers.

Goldfish kept in warm, sheltered rooms are fed sparingly. Change 30% to 40% of their water every eight to ten days.

Continue checking the health of your goldfish on a regular basis.

And finally, this is the time to repair all of your tools and equipment (nets, tanks, filter systems, etc.).

ORNAMENTAL
CARP

TOP AND BOTTOM: Taisho Shanshoku

INTRODUCTION

COMMERCIAL AND ORNAMENTAL FISH

In some areas of the world, including Europe, carp are one of the major freshwater fishes, equally important for sport and commercial fishing. The United States, in general, has a totally different approach to carp. There are regions where people have been using any means available to wipe out the fish. Whole carp populations in rivers and lakes have at times been poisoned in order to stock those same waters with trout. The justification given for such action is that carp are supposedly not true sport fish and that their meat is too fatty for human consumption.

According to experts, some 400,000 metric tons of carp are bred and caught every year throughout the world. Carp breeding and raising is not prevalent just in Europe; carp cultivation is a major industry in China, Indonesia, and the Near East, especially in Israel, and occurs in America, Africa, and Australia.

There are four subspecies of carp: The European/Transcaucasian carp, the Central Asian carp, the Far Eastern (Chinese) carp, and, lastly, the Vietnamese carp. The validity of a fifth subspecies, the so-called Indonesian carp, has yet to be determined. Among other features, the subspecies are distinguished from one another by various numbers of flexible fin rays in the dorsal fin, different scale formulae, and various numbers of vertebrae. Also, the diameter of the eyes and the length of the barbels around the mouth vary among the subspecies.

TOP: Young ornamental carp with interesting coloration (from a German breeder)
BOTTOM: Raigo, a tricolored ornamental carp (above) and a gray-yellow ornamental carp (below)

Domestication of the European carp began more than a thousand years ago. The Far Eastern variety, on the other hand, has already been kept as pets for two thousand years! The principle goal of early carp breeders was to develop domestic carp with a rapid growth rate and efficient utilization of food. Modern breeders are aiming for carp which are suitable for large-scale industrial cultivation and are characterized by fewer scales and bones, and by increased resistance to disease.

The majority of these breeding goals have been achieved. For example, a three-year-old wild carp is relatively scrawny, weighing only 14 to 17 ounces (ca. 400–500 grams), while the majority of the hybrid varieties attain 2½ to 3¼ pounds (1100–1500 grams) by that age.

Centuries of breeding have created numerous carp varieties differing in shape and color. It is perhaps enough to mention the arched-back silver or mirror carp so highly esteemed in Europe. The Tjiko variety raised in Indonesia is a dwarf, reaching maturity at a length of 5 inches (12.5 centimeters) and a weight of a little over an ounce (36 grams).

The differences among cultures, customs, and personal preferences have had their effect on carp as well. Central European people prefer carp of a market size of approximately 2 to 3 pounds (1000–1500 grams); the preferred weight in the Soviet Union is 12 to 14 ounces (350–400 grams); in China, it is 9 to 18 ounces (250–500 grams); in Indonesia 2 to 5 ounces (50–150 grams), in Israel 2 to 35 ounces (600–1000 grams), and in Nigeria 10 to 18 ounces (300–500 grams).

The larger the carp, the higher the percentage of meat. For example, the filet portion of a two-year-old fish weighing 10 ounces (280 grams) is only 42% of the total weight—the rest is unsuitable for human consumption. By contrast, 60%–70% of a fish weighing several kilograms is pure filet.

The life expectancy of carp is usually put at 25 to 30 years. The maximum age is probably 35 to 40 years although there are records of carp supposedly having reached ages of 44, 47, even 200 years.

The weight of an adult, sexually mature carp is normally 13 to 18 pounds (6–8 kilograms). However, individuals with weights and lengths of 46 to 58 pounds (21–26.5 kilograms) and 41 to 42 inches (103–106 centimeters) have been found.

Carp are predominantly freshwater fish, but are sometimes found in brackish waters, in river deltas, or in less saline seas (0.9%–1.2% salt) such as the Caspian Sea, the Black Sea, and the Sea of Azov. But carp are believed to breed only in water with a maximum salt content of 0.2%. The lakes and streams of the United States and Europe are, with a few exceptions, very well suited for this introduced species.

Carp feed and develop best at 70°–73°F (21°–23°C). They can tolerate temperatures as high as 90°F (32°C), given sufficient oxygen, and may, according to some reports, even tolerate 100°F (38°C). In winter, the fish normally keep to deeper water where the temperature is about 39°F (4°C). They do not fare well in water any colder than that. A temperature of 33°F (0.5°C) is bad for the health of juvenile fish and has disastrous results on yearlings.

Many people wrongly consider carp to be sluggish fish. They are able to travel rapidly for several yards with a single stroke of their powerful tails. They can travel considerable distances in a short time. On Lake Constance, tagged carp traveled 15.5 miles (25 kilometers) within 24 hours. However, carp are not known for migrating over large distances. The normal radius of a carp's territory has been determined by scientists to be only a few miles, at most.

In his 1887 book on Hungarian fish hatcheries, Otto Hermann described carp as follows:

"Carp love slow-moving, generally calm, muddy bodies of water where they stand on their heads to forage in the mud in search of food. Their food consists of insects, snails, worms, and even plants, especially young shoots, roots, and · leaves. During the winter, they congregate in groups and dig hollows on the lake or river bottom, but they do not crowd together. During this time, they do not feed nor do they lose any noticeable weight. If spring is warm, the carp begin to spawn in May; they seek out calm, shallow waters, preferably with abundant plant growth on which they lay hundreds of thousands of eggs. Carp are hardy fish that may be transported over great distances; they are not sensitive to the water and grow at an amazing rate when conditions are favorable."

POPULAR PETS

Ornamental carp became pets much later than goldfish, although raising carp as a pastime and hobby was widespread as early as the fifth and sixth centuries B.C. According to historical sources, there were already five different varieties of carp in Japan during the third and fourth centuries B.C.

While goldfish and their derived varieties originated in China, the original home of ornamental carp and their varieties is Japan.

The Japanese have several names for the variously colored carp, including mishikigoi, higoi, and irogoi. Most often, however, they are simply called "koi," which means "love." Ornamental carp have become popular in the United States and Europe.

Ornamental carp come from the Japanese region of Yamakoshi in the central and northern part of the island of Honshu. It was there that people first succeeded in selectively breeding different carp varieties from the original grayish-brown wild carp. Winters in that region are notoriously long and cold; for that reason, the beautiful "koi" were allowed to spend the winter inside people's houses, much as tropical

Tancho Kohaku

houseplants would in America. Ornamental carp have been known in the United States and Europe for only a few decades, having gained popularity in the past few years in the wake of the increased popularity of ornamental backyard ponds. Ornamental carp are very hardy and are adaptable to a wide range of conditions. They withstand heat by day and cold at night without signs of stress, and they are not bothered by having to go hungry for a few days.

CLASSIFICATION AND ANATOMY

The ornamental carp is derived from the common carp (*Cyprinus carpio* Linnaeus 1758). Carp belong to the superorder of true bony fishes (Teleostei), the order of Cypriniformes, the suborder of carplike fishes (Cyprinoidei), the family of carp (Cyprinidae), and the carp genus *Cyprinus*.

The scale formula for ornamental carp is as follows:

$$35 - \frac{5}{5-6} - 41$$

The fin formulae is: D 3–4/16–22; C 17–19; A 3/5–6; P 1/15–16; V 1–2/8–9. See page 19 for an explanation of these systems of classification.

Ornamental carp, like goldfish, have round cycloid scales. When fully grown, a carp may be covered with 1100 to 1200 scales. In addition to the scaled carp, there are the so-called mirror carp and common carp; the mirror type has scales only along the dorsal and lateral lines.

Their mouths are terminal and centered. On either side of the mouth there is one long and one short barbel.

VARIETIES OF CARP

Strangely, ornamental carp are not exactly the cheapest sort of fish. To a large extent, individual prices depend on coloration and markings. Their place of origin is also significant. If you buy Japanese carp, for example, you pay a high price for the fish plus a high price for shipping.

Nearly 100 million ornamental carp are hatched, reared, and marketed in Japan every year. Japan also offers a few carp of such exquisite appearance that a single fish may easily change hands for $1000. In "beauty contests" for ornamental carp, held quite frequently in Japan, the value of a winning fish may exceed $15,000. Naturally, such sums are not paid on the basis of beauty alone, but also on account of the considerable value of the specimen for future breeding.

There are unicolored, bicolored, tricolored, and multicolored varieties of carp.

Unicolored varieties:

Ohgon – golden
Yamabuki Ohgon – golden-yellow
Nezu Ohgon – silver-gray with dark scales on the dorsal and lateral lines
Hi Ohgon – orange-red
Platinum Ohgon – platinum-colored or white (there is a scaled as well as a mirror variety)
Ginbo – silver
Gin Kabuto – with silver hood

Kin Kabuto – with golden hood
Ki Goi – yellow
Ki Matsuba – yellow with pine-cone patterned scales
Cha Goi – brown with pigmented scales on the dorsal and lateral lines
Koshino Hisoku – green (the back of this variety is greenish-yellow, the sides are orange)
Karasu Goi – black
Kagami Goi – mirror or silver carp, with pigmented scales on the dorsal and lateral lines
Shiro Muji – white
Beni Goi – orange
Aka Hajiro – red with white fins

Bicolored varieties:

Kohaku – with red and white blotches
Tancho Kohaku – red and white with red cap
Shiro Bekko – calico black and white
Ki Bekko – with a yellow body and black blotches
Shiro Utsuri – shiny calico black and white
Hi Utsuri – calico black and red, shiny

Tricolored varieties:

Tancho Sanshoku – calico black and white, with a red cap
Taisho Sanshoku – calico black, white, and red

MAINTENANCE AND CARE OF ORNAMENTAL CARP

CONTAINERS AND WATER

Ornamental carp require quite a bit of space because they grow to the considerable size of 12 to 20 inches (30–50 centimeters).

They may be kept in aquariums, but this is not the ideal. A mature individual of 16 to 20 inches (40–50 centimeters) requires at least 65 to 75 gallons (ca. 250–300 liters) of water. As a rule of thumb, figure on 5 liters (quarts) of water for every ½ inch (1 centimeter) of "fish." Since you would need huge aquariums, it is really cheaper and easier to keep ornamental carp in garden ponds.

A garden pond for carp should be located where it will be exposed to minimal or no sunlight. The best place is one shaded by deciduous trees. This prevents the water from turning green and keeps algal growth down. There are also numerous preparations such as TetraAlguMin which will check the growth of algae.

An ornamental carp pond in a garden or in spacious interior rooms of homes should be at least 9 to 12 feet (3–4 meters) in diameter and have a water depth of 20 to 32 inches (50–80 centimeters). In view of the minimum water requirements of the fish, this would amount to about 750 to 1000 gallons (3000–4000 liters) of water for 10 to 12 adult fish. At a depth of more than 32 inches (80 centimeters) the carp can be seen only with difficulty, if at all. Remember also that bottom-feeding carp can churn up the mud and cloud the water very quickly. Murkiness can be prevented by constant filtration and water percolation. In Japan carp are usually kept in ponds with a surface area of 200 to 250 square feet (20–25 square meters). The ponds are surrounded by stones of irregular shapes and are 20 to 32 inches (50–80 centimeters) deep. Such a pond can hold an average of 30 to 40 carp 12 to 20 inches (30–50 centimeters) long. In ponds of this size, the carp are always "close at hand"—easy to see and easy to feed. In larger ponds, the carp may be too far away from the observer and offer very little viewing pleasure.

For your flow of running water, use non-chlorinated clean water of approximately the same temperature as that of the pond's water. Chlorinated tap water is toxic to carp as it destroys the respiratory membranes in their gills.

Small electric water filters are well suited for filtering the circulating water and are available in a great variety in pet stores. Some of these filter systems are capable of filtering and purifying up to 400 gallons (1500 liters) of water per hour.

Helpful hints for building and establishing of ornamental ponds may be found in the pertinent literature.

GROWTH

Freshly-hatched carp larvae are approximately ¼ inch (6 millimeters) long. If they are fed a good diet of high-quality foods (e.g. rotifers, Artemia, Cyclops nauplii, etc.), they grow about 1 millimeter per day. In a month's time they may attain a length of 1½ inches (4 centimeters). They begin to assume their adult coloration when they are approximately one inch (25 millimeters) long. A two-month-old carp is about 3 inches (8 centimeters) long, and a yearling may be 6–8 inches (15–20 centimeters) long in October, at the time of fall harvesting and pond cleaning. Of course, this growth rate depends on the type of diet the fish have been receiving, on the water quality and temperature regimen, and on how densely-populated the pond was. Carp are ready to breed in their third or fourth year, when they reach a length of 16–20 inches (40–50 centimeters).

During the fall harvesting and cleaning procedure, carp in large commercial hatcheries undergo a strict selection process. Only carp with flawless shape and color are kept and used for breeding. In Japan, these carp are called "tate goi". In the course of our breeding work we found that the growth rate of ornamental carp in their first summer is approximately 25–30% higher than that of mirror carp, the well-known edible variety.

OVERWINTERING

Ornamental carp are not quite as delicate and heat-dependent during the winter as are the majority of goldfish varieties. Carp must overwinter in a pond which does not freeze to the bottom, and in which the temperature at the overwintering site (the lowest point of the pond) will never drop below 39°–41°F (4°–5°C), no matter how cold the air outside gets.

If these conditions cannot be provided, even by heating, the carp should overwinter in the cellar or in a frost-protected room in a large plastic, metal or cement tank. Figure on at least 40–50 gallons (ca. 150–200 liters) water for adult fish.

Provide the hibernation tank with compressed air and change about 50% of the water once a week. A screen placed over the tank keeps the fish from jumping out.

The overwintering tank does not need to be illuminated; the carp will do well even in dim light. During the winter, the carp should be neither fed nor disturbed. Intervention is only necessary if there is an outbreak of disease, in which case the treatment must be started immediately. Refer to the section on diseases.

FEEDING

In most respects feeding ornamental carp is identical to feeding goldfish, particularly for young fish. Ornamental carp are omnivores. The major part of their diet, however, consists of worms living on the bottom of lakes and rivers, insect larvae, small snails, mussels, and other small animals. Supplemental foods include primitive aquatic crustaceans (*Daphnia, Cyclops*) as well as sprouts, fragments, and seeds of plants.

Freshly-hatched carp larvae may be fed hard-boiled egg yolk mashed with water during the first hours of their life. Give the larvae only as much as they can eat within a few minutes. Feed one- or two-day-old fry live copepods and brine shrimp. Week-old fish like live *Cyclops* nauplii and copepodites, and fish two to three weeks old will eat crustaceans (*Cyclops, Daphnia, Bosmina*) and finely-chopped, well-washed tubifex worms.

A carp has a daily food requirement of about 1% of its body weight. Therefore, give your fish only as much food as they can consume within a short time. This applies especially to prepared foods. Live food will at least not spoil.

You can also feed your fish with the carp nutrient mixes used in commercial carp farms. Do not forget, however, that your carp are not food fish but ornamental fish. You do not want to fatten them up. Ornamental carp are most pleasing to the eye when their bodies are sleek and their movements agile and quick.

Recently, various food supplements for fish have become available on the market (e.g. Tetraphyll, Tetramin, Dorofin, Wardley's, for example).

Always feed your carp at the same spot and at the same time of day. Experience has shown that carp have larger appetites during warm weather.

It sometimes happens that people are able to look after and care for their fish only on weekends. What can you do under such circumstances? Can your fish withstand such a long period of fasting? Yes. On Friday, when you get home, feed your fish a little more than usual, then feed them less on Saturday, and more again on Sunday.

When you are away, an automatic feeder attached to the tank can be a great help. You can provide hungry fish with food at pre-set intervals in the necessary quantities.

BREEDING CARP

General biological considerations regarding breeding are covered in the chapter on goldfish reproduction. We will summarize the essentials concerning ornamental carp breeding, otherwise referring the reader to the chapter on goldfish.

REPRODUCTION IN CARP

Breeding Maturity

The males of ornamental carp are ready for breeding in their third year, the females in their fourth or fifth year, at least in the moderate climate zones of the United States. In warmer climates, sexual maturity is reached earlier. Maturity is evidenced by the ejection of sperm from the anal pore of the male carp upon slight pressure, and by the development of an enlarged, rounded abdomen of the female carp.

The number of eggs which develop in a female carp each year is 50,000 to 100,000 per pound (100,000 to 200,000 per kilogram) of body weight. The stages of egg maturation correspond to those of goldfish.

The female's eggs generally mature all at the same time. Given a warm environment and an ample diet rich in protein, a female carp may deposit another set of eggs two to four months later. In that case, the number of eggs is generally less than the annual totals (i.e. 15,000 to 40,000 per pound or 30,000 to 80,000 per kilogram of body weight).

Spawning

Ornamental carp usually mate in groups. External circumstances conducive to reproduction for carp are somewhat different from those for goldfish. Carp also need a more specific breeding environment. In other words, it is more difficult to induce carp to begin mating. Several factors are particularly important to the spawning process. The water temperature should be 63° to 68°F (17°–20°C) and should rise slowly. Fresh, oxygen-saturated water and a slowly rising water level in the spawning area are very important.

Recently submerged green grass 2 to 4 inches (5–10 centimeters) high and with no sign of decay is an ideal spawning substrate. Ornamental carp also spawn on finely-dissected leaves of pondweed, but eggs and larvae do not adhere as well as on grass.

The presence of males ready to mate, and their driving ritual, promote the final step in the maturation process of female roe in a manner similar to that described in detail for goldfish. Carp spawning is accompanied by strong thrashing. Several (3 to 5) males drive one female to the shallow, grassy areas near the bank, accompanying their chosen mate with the upper portion of their bodies raised out of the water, as if "sailing" with their dorsal fins.

Spawning usually takes place in the morning, if the other conditions are right.

Female carp deposit their eggs within 30 to 50 minutes, with breaks of no more than a few minutes each. Then they withdraw to deeper waters and rest after their exhausting ordeal.

Eggs and Larvae

Ornamental carp spawn, especially that of light-colored varieties, already shows by its color that it will develop into colored fish. This contrasts with the green spawn of the European carp whose embryos have only a few pigment cells, barely, if at all, visible. The spawn is very tacky in order to adhere better to plant stems. The incubation period of ornamental carp embryos is the same as that of goldfish embryos, but the proportion of fertile eggs, i.e. of hatching larvae, is generally much higher. This fact may be due to the characteristically high fertilization rate (40%–70%) in natural carp reproduction, to greater spawn vitality, and to the lower lethal low temperatures (54°–57°F; 12–14°C) characteristic of carp.

The behavior and initial feeding of ornamental carp larvae are similar to those of goldfish larvae. They are pigmented even in the larval stage—normally light yellow at first, with the adult color pattern emerging after a few weeks.

HOW TO BREED ORNAMENTAL CARP

Because of the larger body size of female parent carp and the correspondingly larger quantity of deposited spawn, ornamental carp require reproduction methods somewhat different from those described for goldfish. Because they are closely related species, however, some of the main features of breeding remain largely the same.

Selection of a Breeding Stock

Choose only the most beautiful, healthiest individuals with the best growth characteristics for breeding. Make a preliminary selection of yearling fish, then select again when the carp offspring are two and three years old, so that you make your final decision on your future breeding stock in the fourth summer. Breeding stock should have ample room for good growth, and should be given a good natural diet. If this is not possible, feed the breeding stock primarily live foods (tubifex worms), supplemented with meal from protein-rich plant seeds (soy beans, lupines, peas), or with special nutrient preparations. Rapid growth is the surest sign of a good diet!

Breeding stock should, ideally, attain the following lengths for age: first year, 5 to 8 inches (12–20 centimeters); second year, 8 to 12 inches (20–30 centimeters); third year, 10–14 inches (25–35 centimeters); and fourth year, 12–17 inches (30–42 centimeters). Females grow faster initially, but slow down later on. Males are ready to breed in the third summer, the females in the fourth or, better yet, the fifth year.

Prior to breeding, in the spring, the stock should be separated by sex and kept in a temperature range of 50° to 54°F (10°–12°C). The external features of sexually mature ornamental carp are presented in Table 9. Individuals with indistinct sex characteristics in the spring are not suitable for breeding. If you still wish to retain these specimens, keep them with the males, since a male placed among females can induce the entire female stock to spawn, regardless of breeding condition. Feed the breeding fish sparingly thereafter until the beginning of reproduction, and feed them only foods rich in protein. Fat fish are hard to breed.

The female fish's soft abdomen and the milt emerging from the male's genital pore upon slight pressure indicate that the fish are ripe for spawning. Fish in this condition can be mated under the appropriate environmental conditions.

Since ornamental carp are more closely tied to a natural spawning environment, infestation

Table 9. Sexual Dimorphism in Sexually Mature Ornamental Carp		
	female	male
body shape viewed from the side	round	elongated
abdominal wall	widened, soft	flat, hard
anal pore	double, swollen in spring	single, white milt upon pressure
pectoral fin surface	smooth	faintly ribbed in spring

of breeding stocks by parasites is relatively frequent. Adult carp are largely immune, but parasites can become dangerous for young fish in a breeding cycle because the parent fish often act as hosts for the parasites. It is thus advisable to treat the carp for external (crustaceans, gill worms, etc.) and internal (intestinal worms) parasites prior to breeding. This aspect is discussed in greater detail in the section on fish diseases.

The three most important mating methods are:
1. Natural spawning in a small pond with a spawning substrate of grass
2. Spawning on an artificial substrate (nest) in a tank
3. Artificial fertilization.

Breeding Through Natural Spawning

In their natural habitat, carp spawn on slowly-flooding grassy lake or river banks. This slowly-rising water level can be replicated in a breeding small pond. The pond must have a minimum size of approximately 200 to 250 square feet (20–25 square meters), but even a surface area of several thousand square feet (several hundred square meters) is suitable. A large portion of the pond bottom should be covered with grass, and deeper channels should be present in the center or on the sides of the pond. These channels are necessary for drainage and also serve as resting places for the females during spawning. Water is added to the pond by means of a feeder pipe ending above the highest intended water level. Water is drained by a sluice gate. It is rather difficult to set up such an arrangement in larger ponds, and they are thus not particularly well-suited as breeding tanks. Small ponds, on the other hand, usually lack sufficient natural food for hatching larvae, with the result that their growth slows down after a few days or a week, and they fall victim to parasites more readily.

Place two males and one smaller female, about 2 to 3 pounds (1–1.5 kilograms) into a small pond (200 to 300 square feet; 20–30 square meters). Stock larger breeding ponds with one female for every 300 to 500 square feet (30–50 square meters) and keep to a 2 : 3 ratio for females and males, i.e. two females for every three males.

Fill the pond halfway, raise the water temperature to 64° to 68°F (18°–20°C), then add the male carp. On the morning prior to the day intended for spawning, transfer the females to the pond. That evening turn on the water, so that the water level rises slowly. Cover the drain with a screen to prevent the parent fish from escaping should the pond overflow.

Normally, the carp will begin to spawn at dawn and will conclude their mating ritual by mid-morning. The eggs will be clinging to plants on the bottom. Let the water drain slowly, and then catch the parent fish in the channels on the bottom to prevent them from eating the spawn. The next step, of course, is to fill the pond again. Take care that the temperature difference between old and new water is not more than 4° to 6°F (2°–3°C).

The spawn develops in the pond grass until hatching time. The larvae, attached to the plants, then spend three to five days nourished by their yolk sacs. After that, they begin to take natural food. Depending on the size of the pond and the kind of food available, the larvae remain in the original breeding pond for another 10 to 12 days. Then you can take them out with a fine muslin net (0.5–0.8 millimeter mesh width) and transfer them to another pond, where they are raised in the same manner as described for goldfish.

Breeding Through Spawning on An Artificial Substrate

Setting up a spawning tank, catching and removing the parent fish from it, and regulating the water level are not easy tasks. It is simpler if one or two male carp and a single female mate in a small cement or plastic tank (125 to 500 gallons; 500 to 2000 liters) over a substrate of plastic plants or green plants that will not readily decay in water. Run fresh, oxygen-rich water at 64°–72°F (18°–22°C) through the tank continuously. Weight the spawning substrate structure and place it on the tank bottom in such a way that it covers the entire bottom area. The water should be at least 20 to 24 inches (50–60 centimeters) deep. Since carp jump during their mating rituals, it is a good idea to cover the tank with mosquito netting. Be careful not to choose larger netting, as the fish may get their gills or gill rakes caught in nets with a larger mesh diameter.

Carp ripe for breeding normally spawn within one or two days in a running water tank with an appropriate spawning substrate. The spawn remains attached to the substrate and to the tank walls. Remove the fish after they have mated, and let the spawn hatch out in the tank. An aerator and slowly-running water help to keep the water fresh. Cover the overflow with dense gauze (0.4–0.5 millimeters) to prevent larvae from being accidentally washed away.

At the end of the yolk sac stage the larvae must be fed. Ideal initial foods are newly-hatched brine shrimp or the smallest plankton which you sorted by size. If you do not have enough live food on hand you can use a suspension of boiled egg yolk on the first day. Give this substitute sparingly, however; it tends to pollute the water. In addition, this suspension is an unsuitable food source for longer periods since it damages the larvae (fat accumulation in the liver, malnutrition, etc.).

Breeding By Artificial Fertilization

Developments in artificial fertilization of trout have had a considerable influence on fish breeding in the last century. The method for artificially fertilizing carp spawn as first described in 1961 by Prof. Elek Woynárovich of Hungary has had the same impact, at least in Europe. Its fundamental advances were responsible for opening up new research directions in the reproductive biology of fish. The basic principle is to remove the adhesive substance coating the egg covering. With the Woynárovich method, carp reproduction, especially in commercial hatcheries, became much more productive and efficient. With respect to the breeding of ornamental carp, the process has had a major effect in the areas of refinement of existing characteristic features, of breeding new races, and of fry productivity.

The Woynárovich method is now widely used in all major countries engaged in raising carp (Tölg, 1981).

According to this method, artificial fertilization of carp spawn is effected by means of the following five steps:

1. preparation and hypophysation of the parent fish,
2. stripping milt and roe from the parent fish,
3. fertilization and spawn treatment,
4. spawn incubation,
5. larval hatchout and initial care.

Preparation of the parent fish Place the parent fish that are ready to mate into a tank that is suitable for keeping carp, supplied with sufficient running water. Figure on approximately 20 to 25 gallons (80–100 liters) of water for each female fish. Large fish are easily injured on account of their thrashing movements during transfer. Therefore, you may want to anesthetize them beforehand—Preparation MS222 (Sandoz) at a concentration of 100 ppm is very effective. The fish become completely anesthetized within two or three minutes and are easy to handle. The anesthetic wears off in five to ten minutes, so do not waste time.

Hypophysation can take place while the fish are still anesthetized. The procedure consists of inoculating the fish with a suspension of pituitary gland extract from other fish and in suturing the female's genital pore.

Hypophysation of females is carried out in two steps, while males are treated just once. 24 hours before the intended fertilization, grind

Ornamental Carp

dried pituitary extract pellets (available commercially) in a porcelain mortar and suspend each 3 or 4 milligrams in 0.2 milliliter of a 0.9% table solution. Then, inject 3.5 to 4.5 milligrams of extract per kilogram (ca. 2 pounds) of body weight into the females under the scales into the dorsal muscles of the carp. While removing the needle slowly, massage the injection area lightly in order to prevent a reflux of injected solution. This task completed, suture the genital pore with a single loop of fine nylon thread, and return the carp to its tank. (See page 84 for a more detailed description of the injection procedure.)

Twelve hours after the first treatment, inject the female with the second dosage: 3.0 to 3.5 milligrams of hypophysis powder per kilogram of body weight in a suspension of 3 milligrams extract in 0.2 milliliter saline solution.

Hypophyse males with 2 milligrams extract per kilogram of body weight at this time. From this point on, keep both sexes together in the containers. The water temperature should be 68° to 72°F (20°–22°C), and neither temperature nor oxygen content should be allowed to fall during hypophysation, otherwise ovarian maturation will be inhibited.

Stripping milt and roe from the parent fish: The females are ready to mate 8 to 12 hours after the second treatment, as the pronounced attempts by the males to drive the females make very obvious. Lift the female being chased out of the tank, remove the suture, and apply light pressure to check whether spawn is readily discharging from the genital pore. Place spawn stripped in this manner in a dry plastic bowl, making sure that it does not become moistened by water from the fish's body in the process. Otherwise, fertilization will not be possible. Strip the milt from the males into a small glass tube and pour it over the spawn.

Fertilization and spawn treatment: For every liter of spawn, add 2 to 4 milliliters of milt,

and mix the two slowly with a plastic spoon. For the ensuing fertilization process, add 100 to 150 milliliters of a solution of table salt (40 g/l) and urea (30 g/l) to each liter of roe/milt mixture. The spawn is fertilized as you carefully stir it in this fertilization solution for three to five minutes. The eggs begin to swell in size and to thicken, so that you must keep adding more solution. Pour off the whey-colored precipitated liquid and add more table salt/urea solution. Let the eggs soak and swell for one to one and one-half hours, stirring occasionally.

The fertilization bath is followed by several rinses with clean water, then a tannic acid bath consisting of 1 gram tannic acid powder dissolved in 2 liters of water. For every liter of spawn, add 100 milliliters of tannic acid solution, stirring constantly. The tannic acid treatment should not last any longer than 15 to 20 seconds. Then pour it off and rinse the spawn with clean water. Should the spawn still be sticky, repeat the treatment with tannic acid for a short time.

Spawn incubation: Place the fertilized, non-sticky spawn in Zug bottles at a temperature of 68° to 72°F (20°–22°C). In these jars, the water flows from the bottom up, thus keeping the eggs in constant motion and providing them with fresh oxygen. At this temperature, the eggs will usually hatch within three or four days. At the end of the incubation period, place the spawn in larger plastic containers to hatch, and make sure that the layer of spawn on the container bottom is no thicker than 5 to 6 millimeters (ca. ¼ inch), to prevent the spawn from suffocating.

Larval hatchout and initial care: Fully-developed embryos will hatch within 10 to 15 minutes. You can accelerate hatching even more by first reducing the water flow for a few minutes 15 to 20 minutes after the appearance of the first larvae, then suctioning the spawn up into the hatching containers.

When all the larvae have hatched, place them in containers similar to the Zug bottles but covered with a finely woven gauze seal. These containers must have a more moderate water flow than the Zug containers. At a temperature of 68° to 72°F (20°–22°C), the yolk sac disappears after three or four days, and the larvae are ready to feed. Initial feeding of carp fry has already been described.

HEALTH CARE FOR GOLDFISH AND ORNAMENTAL CARP

HEALTH AND DISEASE

DISEASE PREVENTION

The previous chapters on care and feeding include numerous references and recommendations for protecting your fish against disease. Healthy, fit fish are less prone to disease than neglected, weakened fish living in poor conditions.

But even with the best of care, your fish may become infested with parasites or bacteria. For that reason, it is essential to check the health of your fish on a regular basis. There are several ways to do this.

Fish should be kept in clean, well-filtered water changed frequently. That way, you can observe your fish easily. A key to good health care practice is to remove several fish to a large jar of water at regular intervals, say every two weeks, in order to examine them closely and thoroughly.

You can often assess the health of your fish simply by noting their movements. Healthy fish generally swim in the middle of the water. They come to the surface only to feed, and they swim on the bottom very rarely. They never wobble, but swim naturally and smoothly.

SIGNS OF ILLNESS

Fish remaining motionless on the bottom, gasping for air at the surface, or rubbing their bodies along plants, the bottom, or the walls are not well. You can be sure that they are suffering from a lack of oxygen, are cold, or are diseased. Loss of color and dullness of the scales are cause for alarm. Reduced appetite, untouched food, and thin or bloody excrement are other signs of illness. However, loss of appetite following a sudden drop in water temperature is not a sign of disease.

Immediate action and medical treatment are indicated if you discover an uncharacteristic coating such as white spots, a velvety film, or minute parasitic crustaceans or lice on the skin, gills, or fins of your fish.

Table 10 summarizes the symptoms and treatments for the most common diseases found in goldfish and ornamental carp.

COMMON DISEASES AND DISORDERS

Infectious Abdominal Dropsy

The source of this disease is thought to be a bacillus-type bacterium. Experts believe that two pathogens acting in unison are responsible for this infection. It appears most frequently in the spring. The incubation time for infectious abdominal dropsy depends primarily on the water temperature. At 54° to 55°F (12°–13°C), it is eight to ten days, at 70° to 72°F (21°–22°C), it is just six days. In a fish population, epidemic proportions can develop in ten to thirty days. During the incubation time, there are no visible signs of infection.

Outbreak of the disease is favored by an inappropriate environment and by lack of proper care. Neglected tanks, careless treatment, and incorrect feeding practices are the most common causes.

Two forms of infectious abdominal dropsy are known, the acute and chronic forms. An acute infection is indicated when the fish are swimming about listlessly, are easy to catch, and frequently show a loss of balance that causes them to swim on their sides or with their bellies up. (However, not all fish swimming belly-up have infectious abdominal dropsy.) Because the abdominal cavity fills with fluid, the belly is bloated and the scales stand on end, making such a fish resemble an open pine cone. Other symptoms include a swollen operculum and protruding "pop-eyes."

Fish suffering from chronic abdominal dropsy do not exhibit bloated abdomens. Instead, they show characteristic symptoms of scars and bloody or festering lesions on the skin.

A cure of this infectious disease is extremely difficult. In fact, most authorities believe it incurable and recommend destroying the affected fish immediately. The best treatment for abdominal dropsy is, therefore, prevention by means of mild applications of antibiotics (chloramphenicol, streptomycin, oxytetracycline, penicillin, etc.). However, antibiotics can upset the microbial flora which breaks down wastes in a normally functioning aquarium, and their routine use is therefore risky. In the initial stage of infection, quick intervention may be effective. Add 80 milligrams of chloromycetin for each liter of fish water. A varied diet rich in vitamins, lower fish population density, frequent water changes or a running-water pond, and optimum oxygen supply and temperature conditions are also excellent preventive measures.

Festering Skin Inflammation

In spring and winter goldfish and ornamental carp, particularly ones that are in less than optimal condition, can fall victim to a festering skin inflammation, erythrodermatitis. Many experts consider the condition to be a chronic form of abdominal dropsy.

A contact disease, erythrodermatitis can invade an entire fish population by mere exposure. It is a serious disease characterized by ugly-looking bloody ulcers and skin lesions the size of peas or larger. The disease is caused by a bacterium but can be checked with antibiotics, even though it is infectious. Laboratory studies showed

that cell tissue from ulcers treated with antibiotics and chemotherapeutics and then injected into healthy fish did not transmit the disease to the healthy fish. The experiments also determined that the bacteria causing the disease were susceptible to most antibiotics, except penicillin and ampicillin.

Typical symptoms of the disease are listless fish, a bloated abdominal cavity filled with a transparent or opaque fluid, up-ended scales, bulging eyes, pale gill plates, a protruding, dark red anal pore, and the development of bloody lesions, dead spots, and bloody ulcers on the skin.

The drugs suggested for abdominal dropsy (except for penicillin) are best suited to the treatment of this disease. Good results can also be obtained with a combination of sulfonamide and trimetoprin or chloramphenicol and sulfotrim accompanied by a continuous rise in water temperature in the range 64° to 77°F (18°–25°C).

Gill Rot

Gill rot, or branchiomycosis, is caused by a fungus that attacks both the blood vessels of the gills and the extremely delicate tissues on the gill plates or lamellae.

It spreads quickly, within just a few days, and is a particular danger wherever there is decaying organic material. A massive increase in algae and their sudden decay, with the resultant water pollution, can also lead to the disease. Insufficient oxygen and summer heat promote an increase of these harmful fungi.

The appetite of infected fish declines rapidly until they stop eating altogether. Respiration becomes labored; ultimately, signs of suffocation can be observed. Sometimes the fish swim toward the water inflow for its comparatively more abundant oxygen.

As a result of this disease, the fish may die in huge numbers—up to 50% of a population. For that reason, measures must be taken against algal blooms as quickly as possible to prevent the water from turning green. The best way to achieve this is to change the old water frequently.

Copper sulfate (CuSO4) at a concentration of 0.6 to 0.8 milligrams per liter of pond or tank water also fights this disease. Last of all, disinfect ponds and tanks with lime and rinse them carefully with plenty of water.

Table 10. Common Goldfish Diseases
(Synopsis of recognizable symptoms after A. Antalfi):

Disease	Typical Appearance (Month)	Symptoms	Treatment
Infectious Abdominal Dropsy	IV–VI (spring)	Listless fish, often immobile just below the water surface or on the bottom of the tank; increasing loss of appetite; *acute forms:* bloated abdomen, a thick pink fluid in the body cavity, protruding eyes, scales standing on end; *chronic forms:* skin lesions	Prevention: correct care and feeding Treatment: chloromycetin diluted to 80 ml/L in the fish water
Gill Rot	VIII–III (fall–winter)	Increasing breathing difficulty, gasping for air; white spots on the gill plates, appearance of a gray coating which may cover the entire gill chamber and is accompanied by bad odor.	Frequent water changes and aeration; copper sulfate in 0.6–0.8 g/m³ (35 cu ft) concentration dissolved in the fish water
Fungus (Saprolegniasis)	I–XII	A gray-white, fluffy coating on injured body surfaces or dead eggs; the fungus may spread to healthy body cells and to living eggs	1. 0.1–0.2 g/m³ (35 cu ft) malachite green added to the fish water for 48 hours, followed by a change of water; 2. acriflavin bath for 24–48 hours; 3. 30-minute bath in a solution of 10 g potassium permanganate per 100 L (25 gal) water; 4. 20-minute bath in a solution of 150 g table salt per 100 L (25 gal) water
Velvet Disease	I–XII, mainly VIII–X and II–V	A bluish-white opaque coating covers the body; later, large patches detach from the skin; listlessness	24-hour bath in a solution of acriflavin as recommended by the supplier.

Table 10. *(cont'd)* Common Goldfish Diseases
(Synopsis of recognizable symptoms after A. Antalfi):

Disease	Typical Appearance (Month)	Symptoms	Treatment
White Spot "Ich"	IX–III	Minute, grainy white spots of 0.2–0.5 mm on body and fins; intense itching and rubbing of the body; immobility, collapse of the fins; oxygen deficiency	48-hour bath in a solution of 0.1–0.2 g malachite green per 1 m³ (35 cu ft) water, repeated 2–3 times
Gill Worms	I–XII (V–VIII very dangerous to young fish)	Dead white areas on gill plates; in severe cases, entire parts of the gills may be missing; growth rate of young fish decreases; and there are dead fish daily	Bath of 8–10 hours in a solution of trichlorfon (various brand names) in the concentration recommended by the supplier, repeated 2–3 times
Fish Lice	I–XII	Flat, shieldlike brown fish lice 1.5–2 mm long and 1 mm wide are attached to the body surface, especially on the back and at the bases of fins; itching; rubbing of body	Remove lice with tweezers if possible; otherwise, treat as for gill worms.
Anchor Worms	I–XII	White stringlike worms 0.4–0.8 cm long are protruding from the skin; itching and rubbing, loss of appetite, blood suffused spots on the skin	See fish lice
Gas Bubble Disease (mainly young fish)	V–IX	Gas bubbles build up in the body cavity and in the tissues of young fish and cause them to perish	Provide shade for the fish tank

Fungus Infection

Whenever fish sustain an injury for whatever reason, be it during handling or during shipment, the tissue around the injured area is attacked by fungi present in the water. Within a few days the wounds become covered with white fluff, and the fungi penetrate deeper and deeper into skin and muscle tissue. Healthy skin is not attacked by the fish fungus. Therefore, you should always handle your fish with very great care. Many Japanese have a handling practice of driving the fish with a hand net into a jar in the water and then transferring them in their original pond water. This method prevents injuries and the threat of contamination with *Saprolegnia* fungus as well as of spreading existing infections.

Unfertilized eggs or eggs that have died for any reason are likewise affected by *Saprolegnia*. Within a matter of hours they become covered by a thick fungal coating. There is always the danger that the fungus will spread to healthy eggs in the vicinity.

Not only physical injuries but also the activities of specific parasites such as fish lice and *Lernaea* can invite *Saprolegnia*. These parasites inflict small wounds on the skin of fish which are an ideal breeding ground for the fungus. In addition, sudden temperature changes and fluctuations also promote the fungus infection.

There are several ways to cure the disease, particularly in the preliminary stages.

1. Dissolve 10 milligrams malachite green per liter of the fish's water. Leave the fish in the water for 48 hours. Then change the water and add malachite green to make the same concentration in the new water. Should the fish still not be cured after this second immersion, prepare a third bath 48 hours later.

2. Use any of the commercial medications, available in pet stores, as directed.

3. For quick immersion baths:
   a) Prepare a potassium permanganate solution in a concentration of 1 gram in 100 liters of water and immerse the affected fish in this solution for 30 minutes.
   b) Dissolve 150 grams table salt in 10 liters of water and immerse the affected fish in this solution for 20 minutes.

The immersion treatments discussed here, be they of short or long duration, should be administered in a solution whose temperature is equal to the normal water temperature of the tank or pond. As soon as the bath is completed, place the fish into clean, well-aerated water.

Velvet Disease
(Costiasis)
(*Costia necatrix*)

This is one of the most common, frequently recurring goldfish diseases. It appears mostly in the fall and spring—that is, prior to hibernation and following the fish's return to outdoor tanks or ponds.

As suggested by the popular name of the disease, the skin of affected fish is covered by a dull, velvety or silky coating. It is especially noticeable on black fish.

Velvet disease, or costiasis, is caused by a large number of microscopic unicellular parasites (*Costia, Cychlochaete, Chilodonella*). They settle on the skin of the host fish and multiply to epidemic proportions, especially at low temperatures (46° to 52°F; 8°–11°C). These parasites may cause infections anywhere and at any time in a water temperature range of 35° to 77°F (2°–25°C).

You can reduce the danger of an outbreak by maintaining a low fish density, by a regular and varied diet, and last but not least by keeping the pH of the water neutral (pH7); an acid water medium fosters the spread of the parasites.

Acriflavine has proved to be very effective in treating stricken fish. Prepare a solution according to the manufacturer's recommendation—1 ppm is usual—and immerse the fish in this solution for 24 hours. Then exchange 90% of the solution with aged water of the same temperature. Should the first immersion bath not have the desired effect (although this is rare), repeat the treatment.

White Spot or "Ich"

Ichthyophthiriasis—"white spot" or "ich" for short—is a widespread disease among goldfish. The name is apt because the fish are covered with small white dots all over their bodies.

The upper skin layers of sick fish itch. As a result, the infected fish often rub their bodies against plants and on the bottom of the tank or pond. Weakness, sluggishness, and collapsing fins are additional typical manifestations of the disease. It is thus easily identified by its symptoms.

White spot is caused by spherical, unicellular parasites classified as protozoans, chiefly *Ichthyophtyrius multifiliis*. Whenever the population of fish is too dense, or water flow is insufficient, or favorable (for the parasite) temperature conditions exist, white spot is apt to show up sooner or later.

Malachite green is *very* effective against "ich." It is applied at a concentration of 0.1 to 0.2 ppm (0.1–0.2 g per m³). The water turns light green just from this small amount of malachite green; larger doses turn the water dark blue-green and are toxic to the fish. Treat the fish for 10 days, replacing part of the water with clean water of the same temperature and same concentration of medication every two days. For continued protection, repeat the treatment one more time. There are other commercial preparations, all effective against white spot.

Gill Worms

Gill worms, also called gill fluke (*Dactylogyrus*) and skin fluke (*Gyrodactylus*), is a parasite infestation caused by small flukes (worms) 0.5 to 1.0 millimeters long, barely visible to the naked eye, on the gills and gill lamellae (gill folds) of affected fish. You can recognize the presence of these worms by the rapid respiration of the fish and by the white coloration of a portion of the gill plates.

The infection can be successfully countered by a 0.5–1 ppm (0.5–1 g per m³) solution of trichlorophon, (available as Dylox or Dipterx, to name just two), or Paratox or other commercial preparation. This treatment should eliminate the parasites completely. After eight to ten hours, replace the water with clean, aged water.

Fish Lice or Carp Lice

Fish lice, or argulosis, is caused by an external parasite easily recognized by its characteristically flattened body with an adult size of 7 or 8 millimeters. The parasite is not really a louse at all but a copepod crustacean which easily attaches itself to the skin of fishes. It swims in water only as long as it takes to find a suitable host, and is usually introduced into a goldfish tank with live plankton.

An infestation of this parasite produces an intense itching as the fish lice suck blood and tissue fluids from the host fish. Moreover, the resulting wounds offer an excellent environment for other disease carriers, most of all *Saprolegnia* fungus.

Trichlorophon and other commercial anti-parasite preparations have proved to be effective against fish lice. Dissolve 0.5 to 1.0 grams of one of the chemicals per 35 cubic feet (1 cubic meter) of water and treat the fish for 10 hours. Change the water following the immersion treatment. It is a good idea to repeat this treatment 5–6 weeks later to kill any larvae of the fish lice that may have hatched in the meantime.

Since the prescribed chemicals also destroy zooplankton organisms living in the water, in other words the normal food supply of some fish, you'll have to restock the tank with live food after the final water change.

Fish lice

Gill parasites (*Dactylogyrus*) on left, *Gyrodactylus* on right

Anchor Worm

Anchor worm, or lernaeosis, is also caused by a crustacean—another copepod species to be exact, even though the wormlike parasites do not resemble crustaceans. Their bodies are elongated and are characterized by a double egg sac and tentacle-like appendages on the posterior part of their bodies.

With these copepods species (*Lernaea esconia* and *L. cyprinacea* chiefly) only the females attach themselves to the skin of the fish, in which they actually anchor themselves—thus the popular name of "anchor worm". In this situation the parasites destroy an ever increasing portion of the host fish's tissues while sucking the fish's blood and lymphatic fluids at the same time.

With a little bit of experience you can easily recognize the presence of these parasites. Affected fish are listless and lose their appetites. Their bodies are covered with bloody or blood-suffused wounds, and threadlike tentacles 4 to 8 millimeters (more than ¼ inch) long are projecting from those wounds. You can easily get a hold of these tentacles, which are actually the tail ends of the parasites, with your fingernails or with tweezers, and extract the entire parasite. After this simple intervention, the fish begin to

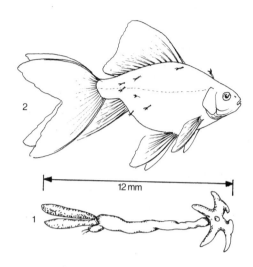

Anchor worm (lernaeosis): 1) the crustacean causing the disease (yolk sac on the left, attachment organs on the right); 2) fish infested by these parasites

improve considerably. However, only a pesticide treatment can offer total and certain recovery. Treat the fish as you would for fish lice.

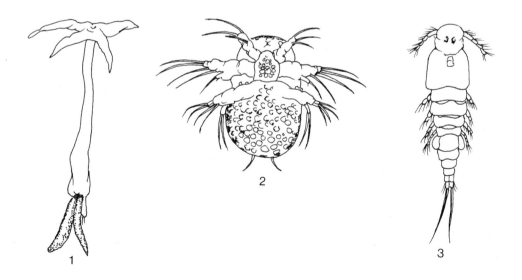

1) *Lernaea cyprinacea* (female); 2) *Lernaea c.* nauplius 3) *Lernaea c.* copepodite

Gas Bubble Disease (Emphysematosis)

Although this disease, also known as emphysematosis, is not quite as common as some of the others, it should at least be mentioned.

In tanks with abundant growth of aquatic plants—unicellular algae and pondweed—the vegetation may occasionally produce so much oxygen that the water is supersaturated. The oxygen surplus increases the partial pressure of gas in the water. On the other hand, oxygen production usually decreases substantially in the afternoon, and ceases in the evening. This causes a decrease in gas pressure. Fish sometimes have trouble equalizing these rapid pressure variations "synchronously," with the result that the gas pressure in their own body increases and causes small gas bubbles to develop in their blood and lymphatic fluid. This effect is readily recognizable, particularly in young goldfish, since the tiny gas bubbles are clearly visible through the fish's transparent bodies. Affected fish swim awkwardly, and their fins become frayed.

As a preventive measure against this disease, protect tanks from direct sun exposure, so that plants assimilate less light and carbon dioxide and therefore produce less oxygen. This artificial curb on oxygen production is sufficient to prevent the formation of gas bubbles inside your fish.

Chlorine Poisoning

In most cities, the drinking water is disinfected with chlorine (Cl_2). Tap water usually has a free chlorine content of 0.2 to 0.4 milligrams per liter, which is toxic to fish. Chlorine destroys the extremely sensitive respiratory membranes of gills, resulting in eventual suffocation of the fish. That is the reason why goldfish should never be placed in fresh tap water. Instead, water has to be aged or "air-cured" first. If the water is left to stand for 24–48 hours at room temperature, the chlorine will all have dissipated. You can also remove chlorine by boiling and then cooling the water. Finally, water passed through activated charcoal also loses its chlorine.

Intestinal Inflammation

Dietary deficiencies or the wrong foods can cause intestinal inflammation, abnormal growth, accumulation of body fats, and so forth. To avoid these problems, feed your fish regularly, and give them a varied, preferably natural diet whenever possible. Feed your fish artificial commercial foods only as supplements to live food.

Starchy grains (e.g. corn, rye, rice, etc.) should be fed only in limited quantities to goldfish (carp eat more). Otherwise, the goldfish will get too fat, a condition which usually causes infertility. In addition, avoid mouldy or spoiled foods since they may easily prove fatal to your fish, or at least cause serious intestinal inflammations.

DISINFECTION

Following a successful treatment of any disease, it is extremely important to disinfect everything thoroughly. The same disinfection process is required every fall at the end of a breeding period.

Disinfect all goldfish aquariums, bowls, tanks, and ponds carefully as described before. After disinfecting, rinse the containers thoroughly with water. Let outdoor tanks and ponds dry completely after disinfecting and rinsing, and do not refill them with water until the next spring.

LIST OF TABLES

INDEX

Index

Index

Index

Index